D0537187

10·5·77

Espionage, the covert gathering of information, is a sinister, dangerous and glamorous business which has been the subject of fascinated speculation through the ages. Intelligence, its organized form, has been called the second oldest profession, and its links with the oldest run from Rahab to Mata Hari and beyond. In this vivid and wide-ranging history Major Jock Haswell, officially employed as the Author for Service Intelligence, reviews the heterogeneous cast of men and women — heroic, bizarre, gifted, mercenary, psychopathic—who have achieved fame or notoriety as spies, together with their handlers, the spymasters, from the dawn of history to the present day. He shows how through the centuries only the technology has progressed, while the principles and motives remain unchanged, drawing together the most disparate characters into the same pattern. From the time when intelligence reports were written in cuneiform script on clay tablets to the microdot and 'burst transmission' of today; from Alexander the Great's 'baton-and-scroll' cipher to the spy satellites now in orbit above us, *Spies and Spymasters* reveals the continuity and ramifications of a strange, complicated and extraordinary world.

JOCK HASWELL

Spies and Spymasters
A concise history of intelligence

with 113 illustrations

THAMES AND HUDSON

For Jackie Baldick

(because it was her idea)

Printed in Great Britain by
Butler & Tanner Ltd, Frome and London

Contents

Author's note

A book of this length, on so vast a subject, can be little more than an introduction. The number of published and unpublished works on spies, espionage and intelligence is enormous, and, inevitably, in this one there are many gaps and omissions. This also applies to the bibliography, though I have made an attempt to produce some sort of a guide for those who may want more information on specific subjects or particular people.

I am extremely grateful to Major Stanley T. Winarski, US Army, for a mass of information on American intelligence history, to John Landolt who sought and found pictures in America, to Denny Jago, Angus Southwood and Fred Harding, whose help was invaluable, and especially to Michael Perrett-Young who took the time and trouble to trudge all through the script and give me the right advice. Bill Leary gave me access to the archives of the Intelligence Corps, Brenda Cope and Mrs Grace obtained vital source material, Mr Richard Walker produced photographs of illustrations that improved on the originals, and it was Jackie Baldick who had the idea of writing the book in the first place.

Lyminge 1977   J. H.

CHAPTER ONE

The 'need to know'

The earliest recorded intelligence report, dated some 2,000 years before Christ, was written on a clay tablet by a man named Bannum, commanding a desert patrol, to his 'lord' in Mari beside the Euphrates – where it was found. It stated that the border villages of the Benjamites were exchanging fire signals, and though the significance of them was not yet known, Bannum intended to find out what was going on. He recommended that in the meantime the guards on the city walls should be strengthened.

Among similar records found in the Hittite capital of Chattusas was a tablet of about 1370 BC relating to the widow of Tutankhamun who had suggested that the Hittites, menacing the Egyptian frontier, might provide her with another husband. The Hittite prince Mursilis despatched his chamberlain Hattu-Zitis to Egypt with instructions to find out whether the request was genuine or part of a plot.

'Bring me back', he wrote, *'reliable information.'*

A very early cryptogram in cuneiform, written on a clay tablet from Uruk. The 'need to know' has always been one of the first priorities for any society.

Tutankhamun's widow,
Queen Anches-en-Amun,
became the subject of a
secret investigation by the
Hittites in 1370 BC.

In all international affairs, particularly those which involve military operations, there has always been a need for reliable information. Even prehistoric man, setting out to drive an unwelcome stranger from his hunting grounds, wanted information which would reduce the risks inherent in an encounter. Moses, briefing the twelve spies in the wilderness of Paran, told them exactly what he wanted to know, especially about 'the people ... whether they be strong or weak, few or many ... and whether they dwelt in tents or strongholds'. Aware of the risks, he sent twelve men to collect information which could have been brought back by one. His overinsurance yielded unsatisfactory results in that the timid majority overruled the aggressive Caleb and Joshua, who had recommended an immediate attack.

Because of his basic instinct of self-preservation, man is, on the whole, cautious, and he has a tendency to try and estimate the consequences of what he proposes to do. For this he needs information, and if he wants to conceal his intentions, the collection of information must be covert. He therefore needs spies and, so far as one can judge from the earliest historical records, has always needed them. Possibly it is for this reason that intelligence – the collection, interpretation and reporting of useful information – has been described as the second oldest profession. Its association with the oldest profession seems to have its roots in the stories of Rahab and Delilah.

Very soon after the death of Moses, about 1200 BC, Joshua brought the Israeli force to within striking distance of Jericho. Here, in the vale of Shittim, he paused while two spies went on ahead, and since he himself had been one of the twelve spies sent out by Moses he probably gave them a more detailed briefing than the succinct 'Go, view the land, even Jericho' recorded in the second chapter of the Book of Joshua. In any case, his two agents followed a course of action which illustrates basic intelligence principles still valid today.

Entering the city at dusk, when the light was failing and therefore recognition would be more difficult, they went to the only type of house where the secret, silent traffic of men in the darkness would arouse no comment: that of Rahab the prostitute. Since the city gates were shut at night, her house had the added advantage of being 'upon the town wall, and she dwelt upon the wall', and thus provided an escape route which was to prove invaluable. It was in fact an example of what is known in the jargon of intelligence as a 'safe house', defined as a place available to an intelligence service for secret meetings or the temporary lodging of agents under safe conditions.

Nevertheless, despite the precautions taken by the spies, the king of Jericho had an efficient counter-espionage organization which reported their presence within a few hours of their arrival. Security police were sent to Rahab's house. They questioned her, accepted her statement that the men had gone, and left without searching the roof. Having made the covenant for her own safety and that of her family – a classic instance of protecting a source of information – Rahab let the spies down the city wall 'by a cord through the window'. Subsequently,

Rahab the prostitute
provided a 'safe house' for
Joshua's spies at Jericho.
Engraving from an old
Bible.

when Joshua attacked the city, Rahab's house, identified by the scarlet
thread in the window – a coded message – was left undamaged.

The principle of protection is a vital one. Spying is a dangerous business
not only for spies but for those who harbour them or act as couriers
and, depending on local circumstances, discovery can lead to torture,
death or long imprisonment. It may sometimes be difficult to find suitable recruits for an espionage organization without some guarantee
that, if there is trouble, the individual will be looked after. Much also
depends on any particular government's attitude to espionage as an
instrument of international politics. For example, in England there has
for centuries been a tendency to disclaim all knowledge of any such
activity. Spies were employed, briefed and provided with funds on the

understanding that if they were caught they were on their own. No one would make any attempt to extricate them. On the other hand the Soviet Union regards its master spies as heroes – certainly since the days of Stalin. Nowadays, when a Russian spy is caught, his government makes great efforts to exchange him.

Yet despite the risks, despite betrayal and despite, often enough, a rate of remuneration far below the level of the hazards involved, there has seldom been a shortage of spies. Many have been the victims of blackmail of one sort or another, coerced and reluctant and therefore neither suitable nor reliable. Some have been motivated by jealousy or a desire for revenge. Others have been strictly mercenary, and if a man will take money from one side there is usually little to prevent him taking it from the other as well. The incentives for some have been purely patriotic or ideological, without self-interest or any thought of payment, and these are by far the most difficult to detect or catch. Others have become spies either because they are stimulated by danger or because they have an entirely erroneous idea of what espionage is like.

Intelligence is fundamentally a service required by those who have to make decisions and, because there is nearly always some difficulty in acquiring other people's secrets, inherent in it is an element of doubt. The report of a spy may be full of apparently concrete facts, but it is possible he may be mistaken or may have been deceived. Is the spy himself entirely reliable? It is a curious fact that so often in the story accurate information of vital importance has been rejected or ignored simply because spies are seldom really trusted, and also because so many rulers and commanders have been convinced that their own opinion was more reliable than that of a spy – especially if the spy's information has conflicted with their own preconceived ideas. Spies, spymasters and intelligence staffs have frequently discovered that it is one thing to obtain absolutely correct and reliable information, and quite another to persuade people to believe it.

If spies had been trusted, the Russian armies would not have been taken by surprise when the Germans invaded in 1941, and there might have been no American disaster at Pearl Harbor.

The question of trust and the element of doubt have always been, and no doubt always will be, basic problems. They are also the reason why intelligence must remain a service and never aspire to executive powers. The procedure, often allowed to become confused in the past, is simple enough. The executive, whether it be a government, a military commander in the field, or a board of directors, must decide what information is wanted so that a course of action can be determined. This requirement is passed to the intelligence service, which may consist of secret agents, staff officers or a market research team, and the service does its best to answer the questions asked. Since any forecast, particularly of an opponent's intentions, can be wrong, the intelligence service must always differentiate between facts and the deductions it makes from them. In these circumstances it can only give advice, pointing out the possible consequences of alternative courses. The final decision must be taken by the executive and not dictated by its intelligence service.

There are plenty of examples of the co-ordination of the functions of command and intelligence in the person of one man; Mithridates, Julius Caesar, Marlborough and Wellington, for instance, all ran their own intelligence services and made their own decisions. But there have been many others, like Queen Elizabeth I, Oliver Cromwell, Frederick the Great, Napoleon and Bismarck, who left intelligence to their spy-masters. It is notable that those who combined the two functions were concerned primarily with military intelligence, whereas those who separated intelligence and the executive dealt, in the main, with far wider issues of international politics.

Sun Tzu, the Chinese military authority who wrote his *Art of War* in the fourth century BC, summarized the function of intelligence when he said: 'Those who know the enemy as well as they know themselves will never suffer defeat'; and he followed this with, 'What enables the wise sovereign and good general to strike and conquer and achieve things beyond the reach of ordinary men, is foreknowledge.' Even so, relatively few sovereigns and generals in the pre-Christian era appreciated the value of information on such matters as economics, internal politics and the state of training and morale in the country and forces of the enemy. Outstanding exceptions were Hannibal, Mithridates the Great, king of Pontus, and Scipio Africanus.

Several years before Hannibal led his Carthaginian task force over the Alps in 218 BC, he began systematically to collect information on every aspect of the invasion he was planning. His informants were people of the Gaulish tribes living in the area of future operations, and he briefed them carefully to provide him with detailed accounts of the terrain, climate and fertility of the country, not only on the approach to the Alps but in the mountains and beyond them, in the plain of the River Po. He wanted to know the number of tribes, the strength of each of them, their capacity for war and, in particular, their attitude to Rome. He knew he could not fight in Italy without their help. By the time he came down into the Italian plains from the Col de la Traversette he had learned a great deal about his enemy.

He then inflicted upon the Romans no less than four major disasters, at the Ticino, at the Trebbia, at Lake Trasimene, and finally at the hitherto obscure little Apulian village of Cannae. At the battle near the River Ticino the Roman army was routed and its wounded commander, Publius Cornelius Scipio, was saved from death by his son, who later became the great Scipio Africanus. Scipio earned his name by defeating Hannibal at the battle of Zama in 202 BC, and bringing Carthage into subjection. He was one of the great generals in military history and, like all great generals, attached supreme importance to good intelligence.

Frontinus, the writer of one of the earliest military manuals – *Stratagems*, during the reign of the Emperor Vespasian (AD 70–79) – tells of

Left, Hannibal (247–182 BC), one of the first great commanders to appreciate the value of basic intelligence. *Right*, Scipio Africanus, Hannibal's conqueror, organized a number of intelligence operations, including an espionage mission to Numidia.

an espionage mission sent by Scipio to Numidia under the command of a civilian envoy named Cornelius Lelius. Syphax, king of Numidia, had agreed to accept the envoy, to discuss a peace treaty, on condition there were no soldiers in his entourage, and the senior Roman officers forming it were all disguised as slaves and servants. Scipio briefed the delegation carefully, telling his officers what information they were to bring back and how they were to conduct themselves in enemy country.

Arriving in Africa, Lelius pitched his camp close to that of King Syphax and his army, and his first stratagem was to allow a half-broken horse to break loose and canter into the Numidian camp. It was pursued industriously by most of the 'slaves' who, on their return, were able to compile an accurate report on enemy strength and equipment. A few days later the real purpose of the delegation was very nearly 'blown' when one of the Numidian generals stopped a Roman 'slave', peered at him suspiciously and then said he knew him to be a Roman officer because they had been at school together in Greece, years before. Lelius at once struck the 'slave' in the face, shouting at him and demanding to know why a wretched slave dared to dress and carry himself in such a way as to be mistaken for a Roman officer. The Roman crouched on the ground, silent and cringing as if expecting another blow. This convinced the Numidian he had made a mistake. No Roman civilian would dare to raise a hand against a general of the armies of the Republic. Dismissing the 'slave', Lelius then apologized to the Numidian for his undignified display of bad temper.

Resourcefulness and speed of reaction are essential attributes if a spy is to survive.

Mithridates (131–63 BC) did most of his own spying, and with conspicuous success. He came to the throne of Pontus on the Black Sea at the age of eleven, when his father died, but almost at once was forced by his murderous mother to flee to the mountains. Here he plotted his return. By the time he was fourteen he had mastered twenty-two languages and dialects, and was thoroughly acquainted with all the tribes in a large part of Asia Minor. While still a boy he returned to Pontus, took his mother by surprise and threw her into prison, murdered his younger brother and, applying his intimate knowledge of the surrounding tribes, conquered them with a well-trained army no larger than was strictly necessary for its task. He was thus among the first military commanders to establish the point that good intelligence can be instrumental in achieving the best results with the minimum force in the shortest time.

It is perhaps surprising that in the days when few could read or write, and scripts such as the cuneiform of Mari and Nineveh, or the hieroglyphs of Egypt, were not widely understood, anyone should have thought cipher was necessary, but the device was well known long before the time of Alexander the Great, who made considerable use of it. His system was a simple scroll and staff. Senders and recipients

Mithridates the Great, king of Pontus (131–63 BC), made brilliant use of intelligence in recapturing his Black Sea kingdom.

Alexander the Great (356–323 BC) introduced postal censorship in order to collect information on the morale of his army.

The scroll-and-staff cipher, used by Alexander. The scroll was wound around a marked staff in such a way that the secret message could be read along its length.

all had identical staffs or batons. The scroll containing the message, concealed in an apparently innocent letter or report, was wound spirally round the staff in such a way that one marked character on the narrow scroll coincided with a mark on the staff. The secret message could then be read from the characters which appeared in a straight line down the staff.

Alexander is also credited with being the first to introduce postal censorship. The story is that when he was besieging the Persian army in Halicarnassus he knew there was much discontent among his own troops and wanted to discover the causes. Normally, as a security measure, he did not allow his soldiers to send letters home, but on this occasion he lifted the ban, and a courier collected the mail and rode off towards Greece. A few miles from the camp he was met by Alexander and some of his staff. The letters were read, dissidents were removed and wrongs put right. It all sounds very effective, though we do not know how many of Alexander's troops were literate, or how many could afford the services of an amanuensis.

Literacy (or the lack of it) in early history and in comparatively primitive countries is one of the reasons why priests so often took an active part in espionage systems. They were among the few who could read messages and write reports and, being better educated than most people, were the clerks and scribes of those in authority. From their employment they not only acquired state secrets but knew what was going on in other countries. They also had the intellect to assess the significance of what was dictated to them.

The priests of Baal, hostile to their ruler Belshazzar because he wanted to reorganize and reform the priesthood in Babylon, conducted the secret negotiations which led to the betrayal of the city to Cyrus of Persia when he besieged it in 539 BC. Centuries later, the Spanish Inquisition had an extremely effective spy service; the Jesuit missionaries in Canada in the seventeenth and eighteenth centuries were the only people who really knew what was happening in that vast country. In the Peninsula, Wellington and his incomparable intelligence officer Major Colquhoun Grant relied to a very great extent on local priests for information, and also for communications.

In many cases, communications are the spy's biggest problem. It is often comparatively simple to obtain wanted information, perhaps by bribery or coercion in one form or another, or even by overt observation – counting, for instance, the number of warships in a harbour. The difficulties arise when the information has to be conveyed to those who want it, before it becomes out of date and therefore of no value. Many spies have been caught because of their efforts to overcome this problem, and all sorts of ways of carrying secret messages have been devised. In his memoirs, James II of England tells of the time when he was serving in the French army under Marshal Turenne during the relief of Arras in 1654. A courier with a message managed to get through the lines of the besiegers, 'having swallowed', writes James, 'the Note he brought, wrapt up in lead (that in case he had been taken and searched it might not have been found about him) and coming at a Time when the Generalls were very impatient to heare from the Town, the Messenger was not able to voyd the Paper in above 24 houres, though severall purges were given to him to bring it out of his Body. This gave them great anxiety, and particularly Monsr. de la Ferté cryd out with a great passion *Il faut éventrer le coquin!* "the rascal must have his belly ripped up", since he will not voyd it. This put the Fellow into such a Fright, he being just then at the door of the Tente, the peice [*sic*] of lead came immediately from him; and by the account it brought, made us defer our attack.'

Speed in communications was, and is, another vital factor in every information service, and though Frontinus specifically mentions the use of pigeons, most Oriental nations have for centuries attached messages to trained birds such as swallows. This would account for the rapidity with which news travelled in the Roman Empire, far greater even than that of the system devised by the Persian kings and adopted by Alexander the Great. This consisted of relays of horsemen, mounting a fresh horse at regular intervals and galloping at full speed.

Many spies and couriers had more to fear than capture by the enemy. In early times, those who brought unwelcome information to an irascible commander were liable to be executed on the spot – hence one of the reasons why spies have so seldom been trusted. Naturally enough, when there was a possibility of unpleasant retribution, many of them planed the sharp edges from their news and tried to present it in an acceptable form. Another reason for their unreliability was financial. Since payment for their services was often in proportion to the importance and value of their information, they did not scruple to use their imagination in producing valuable material.

Yet perhaps the greatest impediments to trust are, firstly, the innate dislike felt by most people for intruders into what they regard as their privacy, and secondly, the element of the traitor in so many spies. Like the snake creeping through the undergrowth, the spy is silent, secretive and dangerous. We all resent the neighbour behind the net curtain who seems to watch everything we do, who apparently makes it his or her business to know all that happens. This form of resentment can turn to hatred because it is based on fear; fear of what may be known about us that we do not want others to know – even though it may be something as trivial as wearing a wig to conceal baldness. The spy is hated not necessarily because of what he knows but because of what he might know, and what he might do with the information.

The principles of intelligence are ageless.

Intelligence must be centrally controlled, to prevent the growth of independent 'fringe' organizations which may well be part of the enemy's counter-intelligence system. It must be objective and timely. Sources must be properly exploited and adequately protected. If it is to be effective, the intelligence system must be operated selectively, with its aims clearly defined. Otherwise it will become clogged with irrelevant material to such an extent that it will be impossible to come to any conclusions about anything. The information collected by the system must always be readily available, particularly for comparison, because the significance of apparently isolated facts may not be appreciated until they are compared with what is already known or has happened before. Finally, the aims of the intelligence organization must be constantly under review, to ensure they are still valid, and the information collected must be continually reviewed too, because previous assessments may well be radically affected by the latest report.

The success or failure of an intelligence system will depend upon the directions given to those who operate it. Though there may, in certain circumstances, be some justification for planting a spy in a particular place, telling him to keep his eyes and ears open and report anything which he thinks might be of interest, instructions of this sort will in most cases result in either a flood of worthless information or no information at all. A spy must be told exactly what information he is to collect, and the time by which he must report it. This will enable him to concentrate all his efforts on a defined task and avoid unnecessary risks. In other words, his mission must be clearly stated. He will then have some chance of building up a convincing 'cover' for his role in the organization.

These principles and the methods of applying them were all well understood and practised long before Christ was born. Nobody in those early days would have disputed the wisdom of Sun Tzu's remark about the value of foreknowledge.

Nothing has changed fundamentally since then.

CHAPTER TWO

Priests and troubadors

The activities of spies have on many occasions changed, or appeared to change, the course of history, and there have been times when the absence of them has had an equally profound effect. For instance, if Julius Caesar, who made such good use of intelligence in his campaigns in Gaul and Britain, had applied his military principles to the political field, he might well have made his famous reproachful remark to Brutus in very different circumstances. Brutus might have been his prisoner, not his murderer.

Even in Caesar's time there was nothing new about the idea of a spy organization controlled and maintained by political leaders. In the first century BC Marcus Lucinius Crassus employed a large number of slaves and freemen in a network which kept him so well informed during the chaotic period at the end of the Republic that he not only made an enormous fortune but arranged his own election as Consul. Since Julius Caesar was for a while an associate of Crassus, and must have known of his organization, it is strange that the general did not follow the example of the politician. Possibly, like other military commanders of this period, Caesar was slow to relate espionage to anything except military operations, and preferred Scipio Africanus rather than Crassus as a model.

In each of the legions serving under Julius Caesar's command there were ten *speculatores*, specially chosen spies or scouts, whose task was to move well forward with the cavalry or out on the flanks, collecting information about the ground, the enemy and the people living in the area of operations. The material obtained from local inhabitants was often valuable, but when Julius Caesar wanted an accurate assessment of enemy strength and intentions he used his own men who had been given a proper military training. He perfected a system of military intelligence and ignored the need for a comparable service in his political career. On the other hand, Crassus, whose political intelligence system had enabled him to become a virtual dictator, put aside all thoughts of intelligence as an aid to military operations when he took the field against the Parthian cavalry of Persia. The result was that of 6,000 Roman legionaries led by him into battle at Carrhae in 53 BC, all but 500 were killed. The remnants of his force were captured and he himself was summarily and painfully put to death. However, good intelligence

The failure of Julius Caesar (102–44 BC) to extend his use of military intelligence to the civil field contributed largely to his downfall.

is no substitute for good leadership or administration; it is the use which is made of it that determines or changes the course of history.

Although by definition a spy can be someone who merely carries out secret surveillance on a person or place, the term more often means a secret agent employed by a government to collect secret information about other countries and, in wartime, about the enemy. It is a role calling for a very high degree of self-discipline, courage, intelligence, judgment and resourcefulness, no matter what the personal motives may be, and when a spy is collecting naval, military or, today, aeronautical information, he also needs a background of technical knowledge. Otherwise he will not be able to understand the significance or assess the value of what he sees and hears, and can easily be misled by security measures designed to deceive him. Both Scipio Africanus and Julius Caesar were aware of this.

From the time when Octavian assumed the title of Augustus in 27 BC, and during the decline of the Empire which he built on the foundations of the Republic, there was no clear division of responsibility and no proper direction of intelligence. The grandeur that was Rome faded away largely because the waves of barbarians which flooded the Roman Empire in the fifth century AD seized and held the initiative. The primary function of military intelligence is to give warning of what the enemy is going to do, and where, when and how he will do it.

For thousands of years it was generally believed by primitive people that priests were in a special position to enlist the help of their god – whoever the god might be – in making things unpleasant for ordinary people who resisted their authority. During the Middle Ages, too, the priest was a privileged person. His superior education raised him above his contemporaries, his comings and goings were seldom questioned and, as the mediator between sinners and the fate awaiting them, he had access to every dwelling in the land. In fact he had opportunities no spy could ignore, and because the disguise of robe, rope and tonsure was so easy to assume, priests became suspect. Since it was not easy to distinguish between the genuine man of God and the spy or agent, innocent men were liable to suffer when the difference was ignored. Even so, the Church grew rich and its temporal power increased as cardinals, archbishops, bishops and abbots moved into politics and became prominent not only in the councils of kings but on the battle-field.

Troubadours seem to have first appeared in the eleventh century; and no matter what motive or mission a troubadour might have, he had to be genuinely professional. He was required to be skilful in improvisation and to possess a large repertoire of ballads, love songs and epic recitations which he offered in exchange for hospitality; and they had to be good enough to satisfy critical audiences grouped round the fire in the great hall after dinner. A mere spy masquerading as a troubadour would be lucky if he was only thrown in the moat.

The robe and tonsure of the monk provided excellent cover for espionage during the Middle Ages.

Probably the best known of the troubadours with a mission is Blondel le Nesle, friend and rescuer of Richard I, who went through Germany singing one of the songs Richard had composed until, one day, the English king responded with the next verse, from the cell where he had been imprisoned by Duke Leopold of Austria. As soon as Richard had been located, negotiations for the payment of his ransom and release could begin.

In the days when entertainment was strictly limited, the troubadour was usually welcome, for apart from his stock of songs he brought news from other places. Like the priests, and like the court jesters who were the descendants of the men that accompanied Roman generals during their Triumphs, reminding them constantly how ephemeral is man and his achievements, he too became a privileged person. His influence may perhaps be traced in the well-known injunction said to have been displayed in the saloons of western America, requesting customers not to shoot the pianist who was doing his best.

Though priests had a special immunity conferred by holy orders — not always respected — it was because the priest and the troubadour followed callings which, initially, bestowed on both of them the cloak of impartiality, that either was likely to be asked to negotiate or act as courier in anything from a family dispute to an international incident.

There is, however, little evidence that anyone ever tried to organize troubadours in any sort of espionage system. They were, after all, men of considerable talent and intelligence, independent freelances, no doubt jealous of their position in society and unwilling to jeopardize

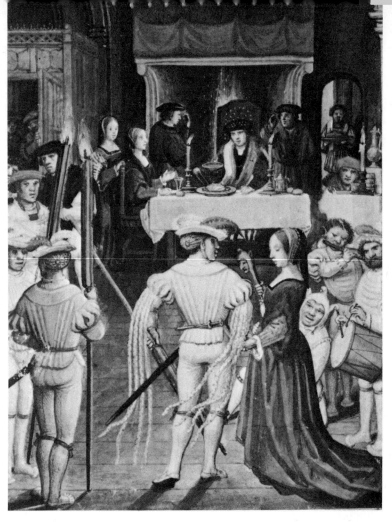

The troubadour, wandering entertainer and predecessor of the modern journalist, had a great intelligence potential.

it by undertaking to do anything much more than relate what they had seen. Priests were not in quite the same category. Even the itinerant friar owed allegiance, however sketchy, to an order, and it was essential for the Church, able to inspire Crusades but unable to field an army for its own protection, to be very well informed.

Oddly enough, even when the individual troubadour was succeeded by bands of strolling players, who must have acquired a great deal of information about all sorts of things, the tradition of immunity lingered on. Possibly this was because the extrovert actor was often regarded as slightly deranged, and therefore harmless, if only because he chose so insecure and uncomfortable a way of life.

While priests became associated in men's minds with wealth and power, and sometimes persecution, in an international organization of which the Pope was the head, the troubadours were regarded as independent entertainers with a secondary role akin to that of the modern journalist. The principal difference being, so far as espionage was concerned, that priests were often considered to be covert agents whereas the troubadours were not.

Although in his role of entertainer the troubadour was followed by the actor, he had another descendant, the herald. The troubadours, making their way from castle to castle and manor to manor, and tactfully weaving into their ballads the names, armorial bearings and deeds of their hosts, became experts in lineage and coats of arms. This was a skill which had a military application. Completely encased in steel, a knight was unrecognizable on the battlefield, but his supporters knew who he was because his arms were emblazoned on his shield. Since identification of the enemy is important in war, the need arose for experts in heraldry who could 'read' the enemy shields and tell the local commander which knights were opposing him. Hence the rise of the heralds as an early form of intelligence staff.

They formed themselves into an international order, and this gave them immunity from war, although each had his own master – a king or a great landowner. The heralds' own coats of arms were a safe-conduct, and they could not be treated as subjects of the enemy or taken prisoner. Their terms of reference were 'to honour chivalry and to desire to be present at all acts of war. To show faithfully and truly business between enemies, and to favour no party in such acts of battle or fighting which is had between the noble men.' Their tasks were to identify the gonfalons of the enemy (a banner or ensign, usually with tails, suspended from a crossbar on a staff) in order to inform their masters or any other knight or nobleman who asked them for information. They had to record the names of those knighted for gallantry, those who were valiant in action, and those who fled when the day was lost. They also had to count the dead and identify the most important among them. Shakespeare's portrayal of Mountjoy, the French herald in *Henry V*, gives a clear idea of their status and functions.

Identification of visored and armoured knights was impossible without the specialized knowledge of the heralds, who thus represented an early form of intelligence staff.

Although heralds were not spies, no one had any illusions about the advantages of their 'diplomatic immunity', and in their ability to make direct contact with the armed forces of opposing sides they were the forerunners of the modern military attaché.

Gradually recovering from the disorder brought about by the fall of the Roman empire, the people of the European continent sorted themselves out into their territories, and the invaders who had poured over the frontiers of the old empire were absorbed. England became Saxon.

Early in January 1066, Edward the Confessor died and Harold of the house of Godwin was proclaimed king. Duke William of Normandy began to make his preparations for what was to be the last full-scale invasion in England's history (to date). Simultaneously, Harold Hardraada, King of Norway, urged on by Harold Godwin's traitorous brother Tostig, started to collect his forces for an assault on the English throne.

According to Duke William's chaplain and chronicler, William of Poitiers, Harold Godwin sent spies to the assembly area of the Norman force at Dives, not far from modern Deauville, where one of them was captured and brought before the Duke. Aware of the value of psychological warfare, William gave the man details of his large army and its resources and sent him back to Harold, but although threatened by two invasions, Harold does not seem to have been unduly perturbed. On 25 September he destroyed Hardraada's army at Stamford Bridge

Anglo-Saxon agents, despatched across the Channel by Harold to discover the strength of Duke William's invading forces, are portrayed in the Bayeux Tapestry

near York. Three days later William landed near Pevensey in Sussex and Harold marched his victorious troops south to give battle.

Halting about seven miles to the northwest of William's fortified camp near Hastings, Harold sent out more spies, who could speak French, telling them to find out the exact strength of William's army and what he proposed to do. They returned with the rather surprising information that there were more priests in the Norman camp than there were soldiers in the English army – an early example of the importance of what is known as basic intelligence: the general reference material needed for planning operations.

Harold, who knew something of his enemy, pointed out that all the men with short hair and shaven upper lips were not priests but Norman troops; Frenchmen did not follow the English fashion of letting the hair and moustache grow long. Acting on the information brought by his spies, Harold chose a defensive position on Senlac ridge and awaited William's attack. William, scorning the use of spies, conducted his own reconnaissance with an escort of twenty-five men-at-arms. It appears that at this time the main function of a spy was virtually the same as that of a scout – to obtain combat information which today would be provided by such sources as patrols and air photographs.

Harold was killed in the last moments of a battle which for nine hours was a very close-run thing, and William spent the next seven years in subduing the country he thought could be acquired without difficulty. He ruled by fear and force of arms, and made no attempt to employ agents to keep him informed of any dissident movements; it would have been beneath his dignity as the Conqueror. In any case, he distrusted the Saxons almost as much as they disliked him. The result was that the frequent Saxon insurrections invariably took him by surprise.

Although in Spain the Moorish invasion was not finally checked until 1492 – at the battle of Granada during the reign of Columbus's patrons King Ferdinand and Queen Isabella – by the beginning of the thirteenth century the threat of any further major incursions from Scandinavia and North Africa had subsided. But it was at this moment, when the states of Europe were on the point of gaining enough stability to enable them to consider their own local expansion, that the tide of Mongol warriors, led by Genghis Khan, swept into eastern Europe.

This huge host possessed terrifying mobility. Sabutai, one of the Mongol army commanders in the Hungarian campaign of 1241, moved his force through a hostile countryside and deep snow, covering 180 miles in three days. Furthermore, its highly sophisticated arrangements for espionage, reconnaissance and propaganda were supported by 'pony post' communications, known as the *yam*, which enabled the Great Khan to receive in twenty-four hours messages from places ten days' journey away.

Although the Mongol victories were won mainly by army commanders of exceptional ability who led skilled and disciplined troops, Genghis Khan's success can be attributed to the control he exercised

The Polos' trading mission to Genghis Khan's grandson, Kublai Khan, 1275. The expedition brought back commercial intelligence valuable to the Venetian republic.

Below, Genghis Khan (1162–1227) recruited spies from the countries he proposed to attack, and developed a communications system unequalled in speed till the invention of the electric telegraph.

over the whole of his enormous empire through good intelligence and communications. He knew very well that information, no matter how accurate it may be, is useless if it arrives too late, and Marco Polo, who in 1275 travelled in search of trade with his father Nicolo and his uncle Maffeo from Venice to the court of Genghis Khan's grandson, Kublai Khan, is the principal authority for details of the *yam*. He saw the post stables, each supervised by a government official who recorded the arrival and departure of each courier, spaced out at intervals of twenty-five miles along the old caravan routes and new military roads, and he says that a single post-rider could cover 1,500 miles in ten days.

Genghis Khan also had an efficient counter-intelligence system, and anyone caught spying on his forces was executed informally and without delay. Aware of the obvious differences in physiognomy between Mongolians and, for example, Hungarians, and of the immediate alarm and suspicion likely to be aroused by the arrival of two or three Mongolians in any European country he proposed to attack, he always chose as spies men who were either inhabitants of the area of operations or who bore no resemblance to his own people. He sent his spies far ahead of his leading troops, in the guise of merchants, camel-leaders and traders.

Against this new threat from the East the people of Europe seemed to be powerless, and in 1242 a delegation of three monks, led by Fra Carpini, was sent by the court of Hungary to make peace with the Great Khan and ask him to stop killing Christians. Carpini was an excellent spy, though he was not identified as such. He returned with detailed information on the strength, organization and tactics of the Mongolian Tartars which he disseminated to the rulers of Europe. It was known that Genghis Khan had died in 1227, and Carpini reported that his descendants and nomadic followers were becoming more interested in the treasures of Far Cathay (China) than in the Danube basin, where the only means of subsistence appeared to be agriculture.

The Mongol armies withdrew, taking the threat to Europe with them, but the lessons they had taught in intelligence and communications had not been learned, despite Fra Carpini's efforts, by the military commanders of the West. They were still unable to see the difference between a war and a battle, possibly because they spent so much of their lives fighting each other that their outlook remained parochial, and no knight worth his spurs tried to take advantage by such underhand methods as spying on an enemy. Thus, in the world of intelligence, the emphasis tended to veer away from purely military affairs and come to rest on Church and State.

The need for what might perhaps be called religious intelligence arose mainly from the attacks made upon the Church by zealous reformers who saw in its power and wealth a complete abnegation of the original Christian doctrine. Although religious intelligence organizations sometimes intrude into the political field, as for example in the case of the young Princess Elizabeth, beset by the Inquisitors of her Tudor half-sister Mary who 'sought to entrap' her, the story of intelligence and the Church is too long and involved for these pages. It illustrates the development of intelligence as a means of persecution, the least attractive of its applications.

One of the earliest medieval state intelligence organizations was established by Charles V (the Wise). He came to the throne of France in 1364, on the death of his father John II (the Good), who had been captured by the Black Prince at Poitiers. Frail in body but powerful in intellect, like so many of the Valois kings, Charles perhaps miscalculated in his assessment of human nature when he instituted a form of police force with the object of promoting the security and thereby adding to the happiness of his people. In practice his plan led to a network of spies, agents and informers, operating largely clandestinely to deprive Frenchmen of their liberty. Since, in those days, democracy was equated with rebellion and anarchy, and rulers were normally despots, the idea of police forces spread throughout the continent. Espionage was inherent in the system, though this form of intelligence was intended primarily for control and not persecution. Many of the great dukes of France were more powerful in terms of men and resources than the king himself, and the throne was an attractive target for the ambitious. It was therefore essential for the sovereign to keep himself informed on the capabilities of any potentially dangerous vassal, and a 'security force' with representatives in every town and village was one of the best ways in which this could be done.

Nevertheless, what seemed to be agreeable on the continent was not by any means acceptable in England where, believing themselves to be secure within the encircling seas, Englishmen were determined to resist any encroachment on their liberties. The problem was the same in England as it was in France, as Kings Stephen and John discovered. There could be no peace in England unless the king was absolute and strong – a fact which most people accepted – but freedom was more precious than peace. Even so, with the English genius for compromise, Edward I had found his own solution more than fifty years before Charles V of France was born.

Charles V of France (1337–80), whose well-intended establishment of a state intelligence organization for the security of his subjects had the effect of curbing their freedom.

CHAPTER THREE
The King's Espials

In the year 1285 Edward I, surnamed Longshanks, proclaimed his 'Watch and Ward' statute, thereby establishing a principle and a procedure which had existed for some time and were to survive until the 1820s. Every community was required to act collectively to protect itself from those who disobeyed the King's Law or broke the King's Peace. Any able-bodied adult male was liable to be called upon to perform the duties of constable in his town or village and, when the 'hue and cry' was raised after any malefactor, everyone had to join the *posse comitatus* at the summons of either the constable or the sheriff. (The 'posse' features prominently in the history and fiction of western America.) The statute also laid down that since taverns were places where evil persons might 'lie in wait, watching their time to do mischief', they were not to remain open after curfew. This may perhaps be the remote origin of England's peculiar licensing laws. The statute brought permanency to a protective 'police' system but did not introduce an information service.

This gap was filled in 1434, during the minority of Henry VI, when Cardinal Beaufort, the chief minister acting on his behalf, instituted the new profession of state informer. The main task of the 'King's Espials' was to detect and report on the publication of seditious bills and broadsheets and, in the currency of that time, the rewards were enormous: £20 and half the goods of any person convicted of the offence. (Beef cost four shillings a hundredweight and butter was half a penny a pound.) There must have been many abuses.

The handsome young Edward IV, having finally defeated the Lancastrians at Tewkesbury and arranged for the murder of Henry VI in 1471, not only encouraged the activities of the King's Espials but authorized torture as a legal aid to interrogation by 'officers of the Courts'. Intelligence, of a sort, was thus linked with violence to serve political ends, yet the system lacked proper direction, there was no briefing of agents and it was almost impossible to evaluate, in terms of accuracy and reliability, the information they volunteered in the hope of reward. Not until Henry VII, first of the Tudors, had won his crown by defeating Richard III, last of the Yorkists, at Bosworth in 1485, was there any form of organized security service which might be described as the ancestor of MI5.

Throughout his life Henry VII had considerable experience of spies. He was only fourteen at the time of the battle of Tewkesbury, and his uncle Jasper Tudor, Earl of Pembroke, carried him off to Brittany. Here he and his uncle were kept under lenient house arrest by Duke François, who refused to hand them over to Edward IV but was determined to prevent them making trouble which might result in the arrival of an English punitive expedition. Plagued by Yorkist spies while he had been in England, Henry felt fairly safe in Brittany until his hiding-place was traced by agents of Richard of Gloucester (Richard III), but Henry had his own spies who warned him in time for him to escape. Chief among them were Christopher Urswick, Recorder of London, and Will Collingbourne, one-time Sheriff of Worcester. Collingbourne, caught and executed by Richard III, mocked his captor from the grave with the couplet, said to have been composed while he waited for death and which was found nailed to the door of St Paul's:

> The Catte, the Ratte and Lovell our dogge
> Rulyth all Englande under a Hogge.

Richard's heraldic symbol was a boar, and he and his ministers, Sir William Catesby, Sir Richard Ratcliffe and Francis, Viscount Lovell, were not amused.

Like many whose road to power has led across a battlefield, Henry VII was never entirely sure of himself. He maintained a large force of political spies and informers which he handled personally, and which was of value to him in his efforts to rule a country not yet recovered from the Wars of the Roses. He attached great importance to espionage, not only setting the pattern of operations against foreign states which was followed by the spymasters of later Tudor monarchs, but even defining certain terms. A 'secret agent', for example, was 'a resident person in a good position'; an 'informer' was 'anyone, often of low birth, who is paid for information', and a 'spy' was 'an intelligencer by profession, having some connection with public calling as priest, monk, friar, barber-surgeon, scrivener or clerk, and without fixed abode, and sufficiently respectable to be a hanger-on of courts, church, civil, et cetera'. These definitions are still valid.

Henry's son, Henry VIII, the pre-eminently self-confident autocrat, allowed first Cardinal Wolsey and then Thomas Cromwell to run his secret service. Neither was able to manipulate it to his own ultimate advantage, no doubt because Henry did not necessarily believe everything he was told. Wolsey was fortunate in that although degraded, ruined and actually on his way to imprisonment in the Tower, he died in his bed. Cromwell had to mount the scaffold to pay the penalty for serving so murderous a monarch, but he had a 'police state' mentality and made many enemies. In the decade beginning in 1530 he saturated England with spies to the extent that, as was said at the time, 'a scorpion lay beneath every stone'. This gave rise to the question of which came first, the plotter or the spy? Where there is excessive plotting there is

Thomas Cromwell (1485–1540), controller of Henry VIII's secret service. The thoroughness of his hated spy system did not prevent his own execution.

a need for spies to find out what is going on. Too many spies encourage people to plot in self-defence.

However, despite the security services of Wolsey and Thomas Cromwell, Henry VIII's undisputed control over court and country was based far more on his own intuition and ruthlessness, coupled with a predilection for the axe and block as the means of dealing with insubordination, than on any system of spies and informers. He discovered that fear, carefully inspired and properly applied, can be less expensive and equally effective.

Henry VIII was succeeded by his son Edward VI, who died before his influence could be felt, and then by his daughter Mary, a devout Roman Catholic. She married Philip II of Spain, a reluctant husband, and largely at his instigation set up an English Inquisition which worked industriously to root out the heresy of Protestantism planted by her father. Her half-sister Elizabeth, heir to the throne and brought up as a Protestant, was the principal and obvious target of the spies of the Inquisition. If it could be proved she was a heretic it might be possible to destroy her and ensure a Catholic succession. During the five years of Mary's troubled reign Elizabeth was careful to play no part in politics and to hear Mass every day. There was very little for Mary's spies to report.

When Elizabeth eventually came to the throne it was obvious to all Europe that England, a Protestant island in the great Roman Catholic ocean, would soon be swamped by France and Spain, but by the end of Gloriana's reign Spain had been humbled and ruined, France was in disorder, and England was a world power in her own right. It would be wrong to attribute this almost miraculous change in England's status entirely to the intelligence organizations of men like William Cecil, later Lord Burghley, and Francis Walsingham, but it is unlikely that Elizabeth herself could have survived without them.

The main issue was uncomplicated. From the point of view of Philip II of Spain the contest was between the true faith and heresy. To the majority of Englishmen, Philip was a threat to their sovereignty and independence. This threat was real enough, and during the early part of her reign Elizabeth and her ministers were on the defensive against what appeared to be the overwhelming strength of their enemies.

Sir Francis Walsingham was not the first of the spymasters in English history, but he was undoubtedly one of the greatest. He was also one of the small, select band who did not use their organizations to further their own ends. His secret service had national, not personal, aims. Lean and dark – Elizabeth called him her 'Moor' – Italianate in looks and subtlety, he gave his health and his private fortune to the protection of his queen and the defence of his country. He was a man of integrity and high moral principles. His enemies were Philip II of Spain, Mary Stuart the Catholic Queen of Scots – heir to the English throne if anything happened to Elizabeth – the Jesuit agents of Rome, and all those who plotted to take Elizabeth's life and restore the Catholic succession with Mary Stuart.

Sir Francis Walsingham (1530–90), one of England's greatest spymasters, portrayed with the Chancellor's seal (authority), sealed despatches (information), a serpent (guile) and an owl (wisdom). In the lower picture he is apparently giving his queen an intelligence briefing.

Because of his powers of organization, observation and analysis, and because of his dedicated pursuit of foreknowledge, Walsingham can be called the father of intelligence in England and the true founder of the departments which, centuries later, became known as MI5 and MI6. MI5, the Security Service, is primarily defensive, whereas MI6 is acquisitive. His espionage was so efficient that Philip of Spain is said to have complained that all his secret plans for conquering England were taken to Elizabeth by Walsingham's agents, read by her, and then sent back to Spain where they circulated as gossip in his own court before he had had time to hand them officially to his ministers. Yet the stories of the great size of Walsingham's network in Europe are unfounded. Parsimonious by nature, Elizabeth was always short of money, and there was little to spare for intelligence. Walsingham was compelled to concentrate on quality, not quantity, and to meet most of the cost from his own pocket. His agents were relatively few in

Left, Mary Stuart, Queen of Scots: Walsingham's major intelligence target before the Armada. *Right*, Elizabeth I, wearing the Rainbow Robe embroidered with eyes and ears to symbolize the functions of her far-reaching intelligence organization.

VGZ1 UVdₜWo 100ᵬzUG
8bθ- Ub oguθo 23 ub
UGo UVdₜWo b8 o3ᵬV
⌐12b3 b8 UGo ⴰHb3o
b3 ó2UGoθ 12Ró

A cryptogram composed and written by Chaucer, believed to have been an agent for John of Gaunt.

number, but they were in touch with the best available sources of information. They moved in the highest circles of Philip's court and even managed to penetrate the Vatican.

Walsingham's counter-intelligence organization was equally efficient, and his security service in England exposed and neutralized a succession of plots against the life of the Queen, the best known being those of Roberto Ridolphi, Francis Throckmorton and Anthony Babington. Not so well known is the story of the young playwright, Christopher Marlowe.

In 1569, when Mary Stuart fled from all the trouble she had caused in Scotland to seek help from her cousin Elizabeth in England, she was promptly arrested as being the focal point of all the Catholic plots against the Protestant Queen. Her uncle, the Duke de Guise, leader of the orthodox Catholics in France, determined to rescue her and, with the object of recruiting Englishmen to assist him, offered extravagant hospitality to English students in the Jesuit seminary at Rheims. Marlowe was then an undergraduate at Cambridge, and Walsingham sent him to Rheims to find out what was going on. It seems that Marlowe worked for Walsingham for some years as a freelance agent – in much the same way that Chaucer is said to have worked for John of Gaunt, and Dick Whittington (Lord Mayor of London) for Henry V – but by the 1590s he had become involved with Sir Walter Raleigh in a plot to depose Elizabeth.

On the night of 30 May 1593, Marlowe received a message telling him to go to the house of the widow Bull on Deptford Strand, where the conspirators were meeting. When he got there he was shown into a room where three of Walsingham's men were waiting for him. Robert Poley and Francis Skeers blocked the door when he tried to escape, and the third man, Ingram Frizer, wasting no time, stabbed him in the eye with a poinard. The story then went round that Marlowe had been killed accidentally in a brawl over a doxy in a Thames-side tavern. Rumours of mysterious and very different circumstances began a month later when Frizer was granted a free pardon for the murder, and it was learned that Robert Poley, a well-educated man who had been steward to Walsingham's daughter, Lady Sidney, had been one of Frizer's associates. Frizer, an unsuccessful property dealer and confidence man, was known to be heavily in debt to Walsingham, who used him as a contact with the underworld and, apparently on this occasion at least, as an assassin.

Walsingham was motivated by genuine love for his queen and a genuine hatred for Roman Catholicism. He did not shrink from murder when Elizabeth's life was in danger. To him, espionage and security were not intellectual exercises to be enjoyed by the fastidious; they were two aspects of a 'cold war' against the Catholic powers, a war in which mistakes cost lives. He was convinced Elizabeth would never be safe while Mary Stuart lived, and since, understandably, Elizabeth was unwilling to sign a death warrant, he knew he would have to produce incontestable evidence of Mary's connections with Catholic conspiracies against the English crown. Mary herself, at her so-called trial, accused him of manufacturing plots and evidence to incriminate her, and he was most upset.

'God is my witness', he retorted, 'that as a private person I have done nothing unworthy of an honest man, and as a Secretary of State, nothing unbefitted of my duty.'

Yet, in view of his exact knowledge of the activities of the plotters and their links with members of the Society of Jesus – banned in England and therefore operating clandestinely – there is perhaps some doubt whether the danger to Elizabeth was as real as he said it was. Certainly for the last year of her life, while Mary was imprisoned at Chartley Hall under the close and hostile guard of Sir Amyas Paulet, all her secret correspondence, concealed in the hollowed-out bungs of beer barrels brought in and taken out of the house at regular intervals, was read by Walsingham and his expert decipherer Thomas Phelips, before it reached its destination. In these circumstances it was virtually impossible for any threat to Elizabeth to remain undetected, though to portray Mary Stuart as an innocent figurehead and a martyr to Protestant bigotry is to ignore facts and to underestimate the menace of invasion, which was Walsingham's principal espionage target.

Mary Stuart, with her French connection and her alleged arrangement with Philip of Spain over the future of the Scottish throne, was regarded as a dangerous enemy although, being in captivity, there was no difficulty about keeping a watch on her. To discover when, where and how the Catholic invasion would come was an entirely different

Christopher Marlowe, dramatist and spy, 'taken out' by Walsingham's security service. This face could be his, though there is no authenticated portrait.

problem, and Walsingham chose his agents carefully and well. Gilbert Gifford, the double agent whose services in trapping Mary Stuart had been so useful, William Wade and Charles Paget were among the best of his counter-intelligence staff, while on the continent Stephen Paule ran an organization in Venice, Richard Gibbs operated in Spain under the cover story that he was a Scotsman and therefore an enemy of England, and Anthony Standen was responsible for Spanish affairs in general.

Standen was an exceptional man with a natural aptitude for espionage. The task allotted to him was formidable, and he went about it methodically and with skill. He established his base in Tuscany and, using the pseudonym 'Pompeo Pelligrini' – which appears as 'Pompey' in Walsingham's papers – he became friendly with Giovanni Figliazzi, recently appointed Tuscan ambassador to the court of Spain. Things went so well in Florence, and the situation seemed so promising, that Standen then borrowed 100 crowns from Walsingham (an indication of the chronic shortage of intelligence funds), and sent off to Spain an unnamed Fleming whose brother was employed as a secretary by the Marquis of Santa Cruz. The Marquis was Grand Admiral of the Spanish navy and in charge of all arrangements for the mustering of the Armada.

The combination of Standen, Figliazzi and the Fleming and his brother produced excellent results, for in March 1587 Walsingham was sent a copy of the secret report written by Santa Cruz for Philip II, giving all details of the fleet under his command. Standen added his own deductions and comments, saying accurately enough that the Armada would not be ready for sea in 1587.

In the following month Sir Francis Drake acted on this information, raided Cadiz, burned a great deal of shipping and stores, and effectively 'singed the King of Spain's beard'. Standen duly reported on the success of this operation and, in notifying Lord Burghley, Walsingham was careful to stress the need to protect a vital source of intelligence.

'By the enclosed, from Florence,' he wrote, 'your Lordship may perceive how some stay is made of the foreign preparations. I humbly pray your Lordship that Pompey's letter may be reserved for yourself. I would be loth the gentleman should have any harm through my default.'

Philip of Spain, in need of money to pay for repairs to the damage done by Drake, approached the money-lenders of Genoa. Standen sent this information to Walsingham immediately. He, knowing how much the Genoese valued the good will of Elizabeth, tactfully let it be known how gratified the Queen of England would be if the bankers should find themselves unable to accede to the wishes of the King of Spain.

Sir Francis Bacon, in his *Religious Meditations*, had already written '*Nam et ipsa scientia potestas est*' – knowledge itself is power. Now Walsingham, who coined the phrase 'Knowledge is never too dear', demonstrated how the power of gold can be manipulated, particularly when it is allied with knowledge.

Standen's report on the Armada, early in 1588, was characteristically accurate. He said it would leave Lisbon in the middle of May. (Philip had annexed Portugal in 1580.) Its progress was duly charted by Walsingham's agents in Spain and France as the huge fleet sailed up the coast, and subsequently England's sailors, aided by weather and rocks, removed the threat of invasion.

The Tudors were too autocratic to be grateful, and Elizabeth was no exception. She allowed Walsingham to spend all his money in her service and then to die in poverty and distress. His successor, Robert Cecil, later first Lord Salisbury, took over the secret service but did not maintain it with the enthusiasm of the great spymaster himself.

It was at the time of Walsingham's death in 1590 that Robert Poley is said to have emerged from the shadows and invited another Thomas Phelips, one of the four sons of the decipherer (who had died in 1588), to join him in partnership. They then opened an agency for commercial espionage, believed to be the first of its kind.

By comparison with political and naval intelligence, military intelligence was of minor importance in the reign of Elizabeth I – except in the dreadful Irish campaigns – yet it became officially recognized by the appointment of Scoutmasters, whose tasks were 'to search and view, that there be no enemies laid privily for annoyance'. This military title was first introduced by Henry VIII and must not be confused with the movement founded centuries later by a distinguished intelligence officer, Robert Baden-Powell. One of the earliest holders, Thomas Nevynson, died on 11 July 1590, and on his tomb in the sanctuary of Eastry church he is described as 'Provost Marshal and Scoutmaster and Captain of the Light Horse of the Lathes of St Augustine'. A 'lathe' was an administrative district of Kent.

In Nevynson's time a scout was required to go out ahead of the main force and reconnoitre the position and movements of the enemy. The verb 'to scout' also meant 'to play the spy'. Nevertheless, it has always been appreciated that there are essential differences between a spy and a scout. The latter is a soldier who seeks military information overtly. He carries arms and is dressed as a soldier. His role has not changed in the last 400 years. If captured, he is treated as a prisoner of war. A spy, if caught, is hanged or shot.

And so, by the end of Elizabeth's reign, the simple system of Watch and Ward had developed into comparatively sophisticated organizations, manned by specialists and controlled by experts, dealing with international espionage, counter-intelligence and the collection of military information on a large scale – with an efficiency which was the envy of continental courts. Yet, unlike the police state methods employed elsewhere, the liberty of Englishmen was at risk only when they, as individuals, threatened the safety of the sovereign. Walsingham and Salisbury achieved reputations for omniscience, and it was therefore something of a surprise to the early merchant adventurers – men like Sir John Hawkins – to discover that by comparison with the Mogul emperors the English spymasters were novices.

An Elizabethan military intelligence officer (Scoutmaster), Thomas Nevynson of Eastry (d. 1590), whose rank is commemorated in a funeral inscription.

Akbar (1542–1605), greatest of the Mogul emperors, built up an apparently infallible intelligence organization which commanded the admiration of such European visitors as Sir John Hawkins (below).

Akbar, the 'Great Mogul' and grandson of Babar – first of the Mogul emperors – was only fourteen when he succeeded his father Hamayun on the imperial throne in Delhi in 1556. He at once began to develop the secret service that became the instrument for governing his enormous country with all its different races and religions. His reign and those of his descendants, Jehangir, Shah Jehan and Aurungzebe, are notable not for aggression and conquest but for the efficient mechanism of administration based on knowledge of all that went on in the kingdom. Akbar employed more than 4,000 agents, and many of them operated their own network of spies recruited mainly from the caste of Untouchables, the sweepers and cleaners, whose menial tasks gave them access to all parts of every house, where their movements were hardly noticed and never questioned.

When Sir John Hawkins arrived at Surat in 1609 the local governor, Mukharib Khan, instigated by the Portuguese merchants who were already in the area and wanted no commercial competition, was uncooperative and discourteous. Hawkins went to the palace of Fatehpur Sikri, near Agra, to see the emperor. Slightly apprehensive because of the treatment he had received at the coast, Hawkins approached with caution but was received with all the ceremony due to a guest and ambassador. In a private audience, and before Hawkins had time to say anything, Jehangir apologized for all that had happened at Surat, more than 500 miles away, and assured his visitor that disciplinary action had already been taken.

Yet the apparently infallible espionage system developed by the Mogul emperors was fundamentally a failure, because it dealt only with the political and civil aspects of internal security. It suffered from the major fault of inflexibility which will always cripple the effectiveness of such a system and perhaps in the end destroy it. An intelligence organization must be capable of coping with any contingency and any threat. The failure of Aurungzebe to deal with the encroachments of hostile Pathans from the northwest, and bellicose Mahrattas from the Western Ghats, or to put down rebellion in the Deccan, can be attributed to the incompetence of his military spies. The result was the virtual collapse of the Mogul empire when he died in 1707, creating a political vacuum which, after a long struggle with the French, was filled by the British.

In the East the great military commanders such as Genghis Khan had always deemed intelligence to be an indispensable element of warfare, and attached great importance to the reports of their scouts and spies. On the other hand, in Europe the tendency to regard the battlefield as an extension of the tilting-yard, where enemies met face to face in 'fair fight', created a prejudice against spies which, amongst 'honourable' men, was to persist for centuries. There were many knights who felt it was better to fight bravely and be defeated than win by taking any unfair advantage that a spy might reveal.

This attitude had changed considerably by the sixteenth century. In Walsingham's time it was generally accepted that the collection of information was one of the functions of ambassadors, peace delegations, trade missions and so on. An ambassador who failed to keep his sovereign informed of all that went on in the court to which he was accredited was soon replaced. The paid political spy became a professional; the 'leaking' of information through diplomatic channels was a recognized form of – in today's jargon – 'disinformation': an aspect of psychological warfare that is a combination of persuasion and deception. Espionage had become part of the mechanics of diplomacy and government, yet there was one essential difference between English and continental attitudes and methods, which stemmed from the existence of the English Channel.

On the continent, where states are separated by land frontiers which were not always exactly defined, it was possible for an aggressive nation to invade a neighbour without warning. Knowledge of the military capabilities and intentions of a potential aggressor thus became a vital factor of national security, and the need to know became a spur exerting constant pressure on all continental espionage systems.

England, protected by the most unpredictable stretch of water in the world, was not easy to invade. Men, ships and stores had to be assembled in convenient ports, and the wind had to be in the right direction. Invasion was not a project to be set in motion overnight; it could not be concealed and preparations took a great deal of time.

All this tended to remove the sense of urgency from English espionage. It was important but not necessarily vital for the defence of the realm; that was a naval responsibility. Knowledge was certainly power, but from the English point of view the power was diplomatic and commercial rather than military.

CHAPTER FOUR

The seventeenth century

When Elizabeth I died in 1603 she was succeeded by the only son of Mary Queen of Scots, James VI of Scotland, who now became James I of England. He was a sad, ugly little man, so obsessed by fear of assassination that he always wore thickly padded doublets and breeches to protect him from stilettos. Yet he was even less inclined than Elizabeth to spend money on intelligence, and the admirable secret service which Walsingham had bequeathed to Lord Salisbury virtually disappeared.

Thomas Phelips did not remain long in partnership with Robert Poley and seems to have severed all his connections with espionage soon after Elizabeth's death. It was purely by chance that he came to hear of a plot to kill James by blowing up the Houses of Parliament while the King was speaking in the Lords. Phelips made his own investigations, thus becoming one of the first private detectives in English history, and discovered the names of the principal conspirators: Robert Catesby, John and Christopher Wright, Thomas Percy and Guido (or Guy) Fawkes. So it was through him that the great Gunpowder Plot of 1605 came to light, and his brother, Sir Edward Phelips, a noted lawyer, played a prominent part in the trial of the remarkably inept plotters.

This should have been a sharp warning to James, but he seems to have paid little heed to it and there is no evidence of any great increase in counter-intelligence activity. Nor was James particularly interested in continental affairs. His ambassador in Venice, Sir Henry Wotton, was provided with a little money to spend on intelligence, and was expected to supply regular reports covering all the courts of Europe. But espionage can be very expensive, and Wotton's funds were hopelessly inadequate. However, he soon realized there was money to be made out of information, and so he set up his own private system which provided intelligence for anyone who needed it, although he claimed he was no traitor and dealt only with powers friendly to England.

While James I was steering the House of Stuart on the disastrous course of royal prerogative which was to bring his son to the scaffold, on the other side of the Channel the first great French spymaster was patiently building up the Bourbon monarchy into a state of absolutism which, more than a century later, was to prove equally catastrophic.

The Gunpowder Plot was brought to light by one of England's first private detectives, Thomas Phelips, son of Walsingham's decipherer.

Armand Jean Duplessis, Cardinal Richelieu, one of the rare spymasters who never used his excellent intelligence service to further personal ends.

Armand Jean Duplessis, Cardinal Duke de Richelieu, enveloped all France in a web of spies who kept him supplied with a constant flow of accurate and reliable information; and although in the works of Alexandre Dumas the great Cardinal appears as the villain, he was in fact the first great patriot and administrator of genius to achieve any unity in France. Strangely, he did it mainly through his espionage organization, which gave thousands of people the common aim of forcing the feudal aristocracy to accept the authority of the crown.

To aid him, the Cardinal had his famous *éminence grise*, the Capuchin Father Joseph du Tremblay, whose success in dealing with influential adversaries cost him his great ambition, a cardinal's hat. The other chief assistant was that romantic conspirator Marie de Rohan, Duchess of Luynes and Chevreuse, who may have been more trouble than she was worth. Not long before he died, Richelieu said that her passion for intrigue had shortened his life. Like Walsingham, Richelieu did not exploit his secret service to his personal advantage, even though for the last ten years of his life, until he died in 1642, he dominated Louis XIII and was the master of France. He achieved his aim of creating a strong centralized government under an absolute monarch. He tore down the castles of the nobility and broke their power. By involving France in the Thirty Years' War he wrested the leadership of Europe from the Holy Roman Empire, and because of his power and his knowledge, gained from his spies, he became the most hated man in France. Yet, when he lay dying and the little curé of Saint-Eustache exhorted him to forgive his enemies, the great man was indignant.

Cardinal Mazarin, the elegant and cultivated politician-spymaster who inherited and maintained Richelieu's espionage organization.

'Enemies!' he said. 'I have never had any, save those of the state.'

On his death, his authority and his espionage service passed into the hands of the Italian-born Giulio Mazarini, better known as Cardinal Jules Mazarin, who had been his secretary since 1636. Though never so great a statesman and leader as Richelieu, Mazarin was an able diplomat, politician and administrator, with a genius for compromise.

Louis XIII outlived Richelieu by only one year, and there are grounds for believing that his widow, Anne of Austria, subsequently secretly married Mazarin. She certainly became very fond of, and dependent on, him and herein lay much of the Italian's influence, particularly during the minority of Louis XIV, though he relied a great deal on his spies. Chief of them was Ondedei, who was rewarded for his efficiency by being made Bishop of Fréjus, in the face of much opposition. Spies were not popular.

Mazarin lost most of his authority when Louis XIV came of age, and though at times during his long reign of seventy-two years Louis made considerable use of espionage as a means of political control, he seemed to become progressively less interested in intelligence as he grew older and more absolute. There were others in his kingdom who followed Richelieu's example, and according to the Duchess of Orleans, François-Michel le Tellier, Marquis de Louvois, his minister of state, 'was well served by his spies'.

Omnipotence, and a very proficient police force, increased Louis XIV's disdain for the feelings or opinions of others. Regarding himself as the personification of the State – '*L'État, c'est moi*' – he developed a dangerous disregard for any threat of opposition, an attitude which had been shared by Charles I of England.

Charles inherited a secret service which his father's economies had reduced to a few dubious informers, and all his blunders and miscalculations, particularly his attempts to thrust revised Christian dogma upon the Scots, arose from his ignorance of the attitudes and opinions of his people. Like his father, he really believed that a king ruled by divine right; therefore his subjects must do as they were told and their feelings were of no concern. In these circumstances, as he discovered, it was impossible to rule, and since there were no longer any King's Espials the opposition had all the advantages.

It seems that at this time all the best British spies were abroad, many of them working first for Richelieu and then Mazarin in the external departments of the French espionage service. Richelieu certainly preferred to employ British agents, because on the whole he found them professional, conscientious, sensible and impartial. He placed them in most of the capitals and principal cities of Europe.

Charles I had little use for spies until his quarrel with Parliament came to a head. He then began to understand the value of 'scouts and intelligencers', although his enemies always seemed to be better informed than he was. In the first campaign, culminating in the battle of Edgehill in October 1642, the Royalist military intelligence organization was far from satisfactory.

Charles knew very little about the Parliamentary army commanded by Robert Devereux, third Earl of Essex, except that it was said to outnumber and be better equipped than his own. On the other hand, an enemy spy named Blake had penetrated the Royalist headquarters and was sending regular reports to Essex. This was not discovered until after the battle of Edgehill, when Prince Rupert of the Rhine, pursuing Essex (who was withdrawing to Warwick), captured all his baggage in the little town of Kineton. Discovered among the Earl's possessions was a brief-case containing receipts for payment signed by Blake. He was hanged.

The most competent 'intelligencer' of either side was Scoutmaster Sir Samuel Luke, a Parliamentarian, about whom it was said that 'he watches the enemy so industriously that they eat, sleep, drink not, whisper not, but he can give us an account of their darkest proceedings'. Based first at Eton College and then at a house near Newport Pagnell, Luke recruited and trained scouts for military reconnaissance, and agents to infiltrate the Royalist camps, usually in the guise of sutlers or servants seeking employment with the King's officers. Luke's salary of £8 a day seems very large when compared with that, for instance, of a lieutenant-general, who received only £3. But he had to pay all his scouts, and £1 of it was special spy allowance to employ 'those residing at the Royalist Court'.

Promoted to the rank of Scoutmaster-General in 1643, Luke began to put military intelligence on a proper footing. From Newport Pagnell his intelligencers went out all over the country to collect information, and they were carefully briefed to report on every aspect of the Royalist forces, particularly their state of training, morale and discipline. As so often happens with intelligence in wartime, his organization grew too large for him to manage single-handed and he was allowed to appoint deputies – Major Leonard Watson with the Earl of Manchester's forces in the eastern counties, Mr James Pitson with Sir William Waller in the south, and Major Francis Rowe based on London.

The King's forces were not so well served. Scoutmaster Sir Charles Blunt was not a success at the battle of Newbury, and the fearful Royalist defeat at Naseby, on 14 June 1645, the last set-piece battle of the Civil War, was partly the fault of Scoutmaster Ruce. He was ordered by Prince Rupert to go forward and find out whether Fairfax and Oliver Cromwell were advancing to give battle. Frightened of falling into enemy hands, Ruce went out a little way, hid, and then returned to say he had scoured the country and found no trace of 'the rebels'. Luke provided accurate information which enabled Cromwell to achieve strategic surprise.

Charles I was beheaded in the chilly afternoon of 30 January 1649. In due course Oliver Cromwell became the Lord Protector of England,

Naseby, scene of a shattering Royalist defeat (1645). Lack of intelligence was a prime cause of the disaster.

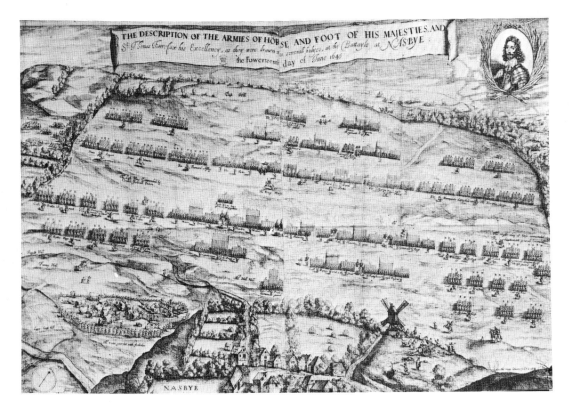

John Thurloe (1616–68), spymaster and personal friend of Oliver Cromwell, established a security system which became synonymous with oppression.

and he established his 'sovereignty' by his two victories at Dunbar on 3 September 1650 and Worcester on 3 September 1651, foiling attempts by Royalists and Scots to place Charles Stuart (later Charles II) on the throne. It soon became apparent that he would have to have an efficient intelligence service to keep him informed of Royalist restoration plots at home and overseas, and in December 1652 he appointed a lawyer named John Thurloe to the post Walsingham had once held, that of Secretary of State and Head of Intelligence. The thirty-six-year-old Thurloe, provided with the huge annual sum of £70,000, during the next seven years built up a service which covered the whole of Britain and most of Europe. Postal censorship was introduced; virtually all letters from Royalists abroad, or addressed to known Royalists in England, were intercepted and if necessary decoded by Dr John Wallis, a cipher expert whose skill was even greater than that of his predecessor, Thomas Phelips.

Oliver Cromwell and John Thurloe became close personal friends, and between them they invented a security system even more effective than anything Walsingham had designed for Elizabeth. England was divided into eleven areas, each under the direct control of an agent

Oliver Cromwell, the Lord Protector: unlike many English rulers, he was prepared to spend substantial sums on security and intelligence.

who was given the rank of major-general, made responsible for dealing with any unrest in his district, and ordered to report anything untoward. Each of them ran his own system of spies and informers, and many took unscrupulous advantage of their authority. Thus the hated 'Rule of the Major-Generals' came to be synonymous with injustice and oppression. Yet despite this rigid system of control, Thurloe and the major-generals had plenty of problems in the form of Levellers, Fifth Monarchy Men, other types of religious fanatics, vengeful Royalists, disillusioned Puritans, and ambitious army officers who felt they would make better Lord Protectors than Cromwell.

Thurloe's success in enabling Cromwell to die in his bed was based on constant vigilance, ruthless oppression and swift action against would-be assassins such as Miles Sindercombe, Colonel Saxby and Major Packer. Like Walsingham, he knew the value of patience and how to strike at the right moment, thus netting all the birds and not merely one of them. For example, when Charles I's former chaplain, Dr John Hewitt, came to Britain from France to instigate another

Royalist conspiracy, he was identified by Thurloe's agents and shadowed until he led them to his associates. All the plotters were arrested simultaneously, and Hewitt and the Yorkshire squire Sir Henry Slingsby were executed.

One of the most ebullient though little-known secret agents of this era was Colonel Joseph Bampfield who, at the age of seventeen, joined the Royalist army as an 'ancient', or ensign, was given command of a regiment in 1642, and two years later was sent by Charles I to 'penetrate the designs of the parties in Parliament' as a spy. In April 1648 Bampfield contrived the escape of James, Duke of York (later James II), from St James's Palace where he was in the custody of Algernon Percy, Earl of Northumberland. James had been captured by Cromwell at the siege of Oxford, and in a most exciting adventure the fourteen-year-old prince, disguised as a girl, was taken safely to Holland. Bampfield was a splendid mixture of soldier, confidence man, seducer, mountebank and spy, though he was somewhat eclipsed by his contemporary George Downing.

Failure of a mission: the Royalist conspirators Slingsby and Hewitt, victims of Thurloe's counter-intelligence organization, are executed at Tower Hill.

Downing came from a Puritan family which had emigrated to Salem, Massachusetts, in 1629, when Charles I decided to rule without Parliament. After the battle of Naseby, Downing returned to England, joined the New Model Army as an intelligencer at the age of twenty-six, and later took over from Luke as Scoutmaster-General. In 1651, after Worcester, Thurloe transferred him first to counter-intelligence and then to keeping watch on exiled Royalists on the continent. Cromwell died in 1658, his son Richard – Tumbledown Dick – succeeded him briefly, and Thurloe continued in office as Secretary of State, but whereas Thurloe seemed to lose interest in intelligence after Richard Cromwell went into exile, Downing sought to ingratiate himself with the restored Stuarts by ruthless persecution of the regicides. One of them, Colonel Okey, had been his former commanding officer.

Though Charles II was the least vindictive of men and had no wish to mark his return with a blood-bath, there was little he could do to prevent the appalling scenes on the scaffold at Charing Cross, and it seems Downing was knighted for his efforts. He was then sent as ambassador to Holland where he had previously been Cromwell's 'Resident'. The Dutch were England's chief competitors in world trade, and Downing renewed all his espionage contacts.

On 27 December 1668, Samuel Pepys recorded in his diary a conversation he had had with Downing in St James's Park. Downing described his operations in Holland, and said that his spies were so skilled that they were able to remove keys from the pockets of the de Witt brothers (then ruling Holland) while they were asleep, open the closet containing secret papers, leave them in Downing's hands for an hour, and then return the papers and the keys without the owners knowing they had been moved.

This represents the acme of espionage and illustrates its three phases: to discover where the best information is; to obtain it without being discovered; and finally to transmit it promptly to the spymaster. The real art lies in leaving the 'target' unaware that information has been acquired, for warning will normally lead to a change of plan which can render the information useless.

Downing produced a constant supply of valuable information, first for Thurloe and then for Charles II. He found that as heads of intelligence, as in many other things, there was a world of difference between the two men. Thurloe had covered every aspect of intelligence; he paid well and gave every encouragement to his spies. Neither the indolent Charles nor his ministers showed any real concern for the threat of Dutch commercial supremacy and, as Pepys says, 'nobody regarded' the information which Downing's men risked their lives to obtain. Like so many spies and spymasters before and since, Downing was that familiar intelligence paradox, the successful failure, during the time he worked for Charles. He could not persuade his political masters to act on the intelligence he provided.

Nevertheless, Downing managed to safeguard his career and his earnings and, unlike Walsingham and Thurloe, both of whom died virtually penniless, was able to retire in comfort to the large house he had built for himself in London – in what later became Downing Street.

The rank and title of Scoutmaster-General did not survive the reign of Charles II. The last reference to it appears in the List of General Officers compiled by Nathan Brooks in 1684, and when James II founded the Regular Army the posts of Scoutmaster-General, Provost Marshal and Harbinger (in charge of supplies) were all combined. For more than 100 years there was no military intelligence organization in England, and the commander of a field force had to be his own head of intelligence.

Louis XIV, cousin of Charles II and inheritor of systems perfected by Richelieu and Mazarin, used on one occasion a technique familiar in the story of espionage. He knew all about his cousin's lack of indifference to women, and in 1669, during the negotiations for the secret treaty of Dover, he felt the need for a reliable agent in the English court. He chose the lovely Louise de Querouaille (or Keroualle) who went to England in the entourage of Henriette Anne, Duchess of Orleans, Louis's representative and also Charles's younger and favourite sister 'Minette'. Louise had no difficulty in becoming another of Charles's mistresses, and seems to have been happy to maintain the great tradition among female agents, that they must be prepared to lie down for their country.

The Bourbon monarchs were absolute and arrogant; the Stuarts suffered from misconceptions about the divine right of kings. Neither House really appreciated the value of timely intelligence in politics and diplomacy. All the efforts of Richelieu and Mazarin to strengthen the monarchy in France culminated in the abolition of it, on 21 September 1792. Exactly four months later, Louis XVI climbed the steep steps of the scaffold in what is now the Place de la Concorde. In England, Walsingham and Salisbury created a system which played a not-

Louise de Keroualle, Duchess of Portsmouth, Louis XIV's agent at the court of his cousin Charles II.

able if not decisive part in raising their country to the status of a great world power. But their efforts were wasted by James I and his son because, like the Bourbons, they could not believe that the monarchy would ever be in serious danger.

Oliver Cromwell had no illusions about the threat to him and to his administration, and in John Thurloe he found the man who could not only take up the reins which Walsingham had let fall, but ride on to even greater heights of achievement. 'There is no government on earth', wrote Sagredo, the Venetian ambassador at the time, 'which divulges its affairs less than England, or is more punctually informed of those of the others.'

Thus it would seem that under an autocratic and self-confident ruler the professional spymaster and his spies will have difficulty in earning their living, but when there is a sense of insecurity in high places their services will be regarded as essential.

CHAPTER FIVE
The eighteenth century

It is most unlikely that the so-called 'Glorious Revolution', which forced that able but misguided man James II into exile, would have succeeded if Sir Leoline Jenkins, allegedly responsible for intelligence and security, had been reasonably competent. He had been able to cope with the Rye House Plot (to assassinate Charles II and his brother James) in 1683, but only because an informant named Kieling deposited all the details in his lap. In effect, James II had no secret service, and in this failing he was akin to Julius Caesar: both understood the importance of intelligence in war, neither of them associated it with political security.

James's younger daughter Anne succeeded her sister Mary and William III, coming to the throne at the beginning of a long series of dynastic wars which, in the end, were to bring France to the Terror and, indirectly, cause the British to lose their American Colonies and win an empire.

Anne was fortunate in that her administration was dominated by one of history's greatest soldiers, John Churchill, the first Duke of Marlborough. He was an expert in military intelligence who, as a young man, learned one of the most valuable of intelligence lessons from the ill-fated rebellion of James, Duke of Monmouth.

Monmouth had little chance of success, but the disaster at Sedgemoor could conceivably have ended quite differently if a spy had been able to grasp the military significance of what, to him, was commonplace. On the morning of 5 July 1685 Monmouth was informed by a certain Richard Godfrey (or Newton; he was apt to use either name of his unmarried parents) that the Royal Army, in which Colonel Churchill was serving, had camped in open country, three miles from Bridgwater, in what seemed to be a very vulnerable position. Sent off to collect more information, Godfrey-Newton returned with details of horse, foot and guns, but said nothing about a broad, deep ditch, filled with water and known locally as the Bussex Rhine, which looped round the camp. Being so accustomed himself to crossing ditches of this sort in all kinds of weather it simply did not occur to him that it might be a serious obstacle if suddenly encountered by untrained infantry launching a night attack. In effect, it decided the battle, because it gave the sleeping troops of the Royal Army time to stand to their arms.

It seems that Churchill never forgot the initial alarm and confusion on that dark, foggy night, for thereafter he made every effort to ensure that his intelligence was as accurate and detailed as possible – with the result that he never lost a battle and never failed to take a town he besieged. Fifteen years after Sedgemoor, as commander of the allied armies in the Low Countries – the northeastern theatre of the War of the Spanish Succession – he organized his intelligence service in two divisions, each with its own head. One, in the charge of his Quarter-master-General William Cadogan, dealt exclusively with tactical and combat intelligence, and the other, run by his private secretary, Adam de Cardonnel, was responsible for long-range strategic and political intelligence.

Cadogan was a first-class intelligence officer. Fearless in battle, skilful and tenacious in reconnaissance, he won his commander's complete confidence by his ability to make swift and accurate assessments of enemy intentions. In 1701 he was a major; eight years later he was a lieutenant-general. Adam de Cardonnel controlled a network of agents and spies which extended all over Europe, and among them were men who produced information of the greatest value. One of them, Robethon, the Duke of Brunswick's secretary, managed to obtain the campaign plans and complete order of battle from the French war ministry and delivered them to Marlborough while he was on the famous march to the Danube in 1704.

Valuable though Robethon was, as a secret agent, he was surpassed by someone whose name has never been revealed. Among Marlborough's papers there are more than 400 letters, sent from Paris and dated between 1708 and 1710, which indicate that the writer was an influential member of the French court. They contain a mass of

Monmouth's disaster at Sedgemoor (1685) arose through the failure of a spy to assess the military significance of a ditch protecting the Royal Army's position. The map shows Monmouth's infantry advancing into the 'Bussex Rhine'.

William, Earl of Cadogan, Marlborough's chief of tactical intelligence.

47

military, political and 'social' intelligence, collected from a great many sources and covering everything from troop movements to Louis XIV's relationship with Madame de Maintenon.

The Duke of Marlborough was astonishingly well informed, but he had to pay for his knowledge. The ideological spy who wants no financial reward is a recent development. The eighteenth century was a venal age in which it was generally accepted that public office provided a means for private enrichment, and practically everything was for sale – if the price was right. Marlborough's espionage service was the best in Europe, and correspondingly expensive. His means of paying for it laid him open to attack by enemies determined to destroy his political influence, and caused his downfall. Henry St John, first Viscount Bolingbroke, and Robert Harley, first Earl of Oxford, charged him with misappropriation of public funds, and Marlborough's defence was that every penny of the amount in question had been spent on 'carrying on the secret service':

I cannot suppose that I need say how essential a part of the Service this is, that no war can be conducted successfully without early and good intelligence, and that such advices cannot be had but at a very great expense. Nobody can be ignorant of this, that knows anything of secret correspondence, or considers the number of persons that must be employed in it, the great hazard they undergo, the variety of places in which the correspondence must be kept, and the constant necessity there is of supporting and feeding this service; not to mention some extraordinary expenses of a higher nature, which ought only to be hinted at.

He set out to prove that all he had in fact done was pay for intelligence with funds allotted for other purposes, and 'had saved the Government near four times the sum this deduction amounts to'. Undefeated on the battlefield, he was no match for political foes, and by the end of 1711 he had been deprived of his offices. They were subsequently restored by George I, but Marlborough took no further part in public affairs.

Harley, the chief accuser, was perhaps better fitted than any politician in England to appreciate the validity of Marlborough's defence in relation to the importance of intelligence, because in his employ was one of the most professional secret agents of the age: Daniel Defoe, the author of *Robinson Crusoe* and one of the most prolific writers in the history of literature.

In 1704 Defoe wrote a long paper which he called 'A Scheme for General Intelligence'. It was a masterly instruction to Harley on how to seize political power and then operate a police state. 'Intelligence', he wrote, 'is the soul of public business', thereby putting into a few words all its scope and value. He had an equally succinct summary of the functions of counter-intelligence: 'For as intelligence is the most useful to us, so keeping our enemies from intelligence among us is as valuable a head.' His scheme was not original, however, since most of it had already been put into effect by Thurloe and Oliver Cromwell. It envisaged a system of secret agents located throughout the country who forwarded regular reports to the government on everything that

happened in their areas, but it differed from the 'Rule of the Major-Generals' in that it was essentially covert.

Defoe also recommended the keeping of dossiers on everyone of any importance, so that disaffection or Jacobite tendencies would be known to the authorities and potential trouble-makers could be rounded up at the first signs of an emergency.

On the strength of the 'Scheme' Defoe became a paid government spy, yet nowhere in all that he wrote is there any mention of his espionage activities, except one reference to 'a special service in which I had run as much risk of my life as a grenadier upon a counterscarp'. This may have been his mission in Scotland in 1706, when he was sent to report on the feelings of the Scots about the controversial proposal to unite the English and Scottish parliaments. Had it been known he was an English spy he might not have returned, but he said he was only an author, collecting material. He did his task well.

As a journalist and purveyor of political propaganda he was less discreet. Queen Anne was irritated by his pamphlet, *The Shortest Way with Dissenters*, and he was fined, pilloried and imprisoned. He complained constantly and bitterly about the parsimoniousness of spymasters such as Lord Godolphin and Robert Harley, who sent him on dangerous espionage missions and refused to pay him adequately for the risks he

Daniel Defoe, writer, propagandist and secret agent, punished by Queen Anne for writing an injudicious pamphlet. His career as a secret agent was both more hazardous and more discreet.

49

Hermann-Maurice, Count de Saxe, commander of the French armies under Louis XV. His theory and practice of intelligence strongly influenced Frederick the Great, to the discomfiture of Saxe's French successors.

took. Perhaps one of the reasons for Harley's attack on Marlborough may have been resentment that the great soldier had spent so much money – in the region of £340,000 – on espionage, whereas, as his own relationship with Defoe had proved, it was not necessary to waste money on spies.

Thus, in England during the early part of the eighteenth century, considerable progress was made in developing intelligence systems as a necessary adjunct to the making of military and political plans and decisions. Defoe set out the theory and principles of intelligence in general; Marlborough, quite independently, established the finest practical organization in Europe.

Even though very few of Defoe's recommendations were adopted in England, the activities of Jacobites forced the government to maintain a counter-intelligence system. The movement of conspirators across the Channel was almost continuous. Many of them were military spies employed by France and belonged to an intelligence service instituted by Hermann-Maurice, Count de Saxe, in 1746, when Louis XV gave him command of the French armies and camps.

The Count de Saxe occupies a position in intelligence history between Gustavus Adolphus of Sweden and Frederick the Great. Gustavus Adolphus was the great military innovator who introduced a command and staff structure which made special provision for intelligence. His ideas were taken up and developed by Marshal Saxe who said, 'You cannot give too much attention to spies and guides ... they are like eyes, and equally necessary to a general.'

Frederick the Great adopted the Swedish organization, studied Saxe's campaigns, and followed his principles. Other French generals did not. One of the reasons Frederick gave for his devastating defeat of the French Marshal, the Duke de Rohan Soubise, at Rossbach on 5 November 1757 was: 'Marshal de Soubise is always followed by a hundred cooks; I am always preceded by a hundred spies ... the proportion of spies to cooks in my army is twenty to one.'

Few of the Jacobites achieved any success, and indeed it would seem that to many of them conspiracy and espionage were ends in themselves, in that they brought glamour, adventure and excitement into lives that might otherwise have been dull. Fortunately for them, the risks were not very great; probably because it was difficult to take them seriously. When a man named Robinson was caught, tried and found guilty of espionage, his sentence was only six months in the Tower of London. Nevertheless the Jacobites, no doubt unwittingly, added very greatly to their difficulties and risks by trying to combine the two quite separate roles of espionage and political conspiracy. Every spy has to take risks, but his chances of success are greatly reduced if he has more than one mission and more than one cover story to conceal it.

Two years after the Robinson case a certain Dr Hensey, a French professional spy living in England, was arrested, and because he was considered to be dangerous, brought to trial instead of deported. Since he was the brother of a French diplomat, Abbé Hensey, the spy, recalling the sentence given to Robinson, felt safe enough. His brother addressed the court, pointing out that a professional spy could not be treated as an ordinary felon, and it was a very nasty shock to both of them when the spy was sentenced to be hanged. Though there is some doubt whether or not Dr Hensey was actually executed, the realities of espionage suddenly became apparent to the army of informers, all over Europe, who had come to look upon the collection and marketing of information as a profitable and safe occupation. It was understandable that the traitor-spy should be harshly treated, but a professional like Hensey was no traitor. It was felt he was serving his country in a capacity little different from that of an ambassador and the members of his staff, and they were not rated as criminals.

Then, in the midst of all this speculation on the status and prospects of espionage as a profession, there appeared an unusual character who was to make a unique contribution to the story of spies and spymasters.

Charles Geneviève Louis Auguste André Timothée d'Eon de Beaumont, known as the Chevalier d'Eon, was born at Tonnerre, about 100 miles from Paris, in 1728, and in the custom of the times was made to wear long frocks until the age of seven. This may have had a lasting effect upon him, or there may have been some deeper psychological incentive, but he certainly became one of the most accomplished of female impersonators. Indeed, it was so difficult to determine his real sex that he was the subject of many wagers. Not until a panel of medical experts carried out a post-mortem examination, and pronounced that he was male, was the truth known. It seems possible he did not possess the full complement of masculine equipment, although, in infancy, there must have been enough to justify the male names bestowed at his christening.

Intellectually he was something of a child prodigy, obtaining a degree in civil and canonical law and being admitted to the Bar in the city of his birth while his contemporaties were still at school. His apparent femininity could have excited a certain amount of derision, but this was the age of duelling, and the young Chevalier, elected Grand Master of the Salle d'Armes in Tonnerre, was one of the finest swordsmen in France.

He first came to the notice of Louis XV when he wrote a scholarly paper on economics, and he was about to take up an appointment in the Ministry of Finance when it was decided he would be far better employed as a secret agent in the Russian court.

At this time, George II of England was deeply suspicious of French and Prussian designs on his beloved Hanover, and was negotiating with the Russian Chancellor, Bestuzhev, for the hire of 60,000 mercenaries for its defence. The agreement was about to be signed and ratified when Louis XV intervened. He sent the Chevalier de Valcroissant to make a direct approach to the Tsarina Elizabeth, but English gold had been distributed with such care and forethought that Valcroissant, representing a threat to the benefits Bestuzhev hoped to gain from the treaty, was arrested and accused of spying.

Russia was very 'spy-conscious', and had been ever since the days of Ivan the Terrible, a contemporary of Elizabeth I. At the end of the seventeenth century, Peter the Great reorganized the political police, a force directly and personally controlled by the Tsar, and gave them the name 'Special Office of the Tsar'. Peter II shortened this euphemism to 'Secret Office' and disbanded the Bureau of Political Police. The Tsarina Elizabeth revived it and, with what appeared to be a laudably humane gesture, abolished the rack as an aid to interrogation. The *knut* or knout, a form of scourge or whip, had proved to be more effective. The rulers of Russia have always suffered from a sense of insecurity and have long been dependent on the system Defoe advocated.

The Chevalier d'Eon and a Chevalier Douglass were now given the hazardous assignment of establishing diplomatic relations with Russia, securing the release of Valcroissant, and destroying the Anglo-Russian agreement for the defence of the State of Hanover. The cover plan was uncomplicated. Douglass was to be travelling on the orders of his physician who, for the good of his patient's lungs, had prescribed a visit to a cold climate. He was to be accompanied by his 'niece', the lovely 'Lia de Beaumont'. By some means or other they were to contact the Vice Chancellor, Vorontsov, known to be anti-British and possibly, with encouragement, pro-French. Through him they were to obtain an audience with the Tsarina and hand to her a personal letter from

The elderly Tsarina Elizabeth. On discovering that one of her maids-in-waiting was a French spy in disguise, she offered him a post in the Imperial Russian Army.

Louis XV concealed in the binding of a copy of Montesquieu's *De l'Esprit des Lois*.

The two agents held the dress rehearsal of their uncle and niece roles in the Duchy of Saxony-Anhalt, not far from Dresden in eastern Germany. They were an immediate success. 'Lia', described as 'small and slight, with a pink and white complexion and pleasing, gentle expression', possessed a 'melodious voice' which 'she' used to advantage in the part of a shy, reserved little thing, seeing the world for the first time. As a woman, d'Eon delighted court society in Anhalt. His portrait was painted and his admirers were reluctant to let him continue the journey to St Petersburg, where, in due course, he and Douglass arrived at the house of a French banker named Michel.

Douglass found the way to Vorontsov completely blocked by Bestuzhev's agents, but doors that were closed to him opened wide to admit the charming 'Lia'. 'She' was presented to the Tsarina, who was so enchanted by the beautiful and accomplished niece of the Chevalier Douglass that 'Lia' was appointed Maid of Honour – even, so it is said, attending the ritual of bathing the Tsarina, and becoming a reader to the elderly Empress. No doubt the first book suggested was *De l'Esprit des Lois*. The immediate effect of Lia de Beaumont's attendance upon Elizabeth was a report sent to London by the British ambassador, stating that Chancellor Bestuzhev was finding it impossible to persuade

The Chevalier d'Eon (1728–1810), master swordsman, spy and (*right*) female impersonator. As 'Lia de Beaumont' he gained great influence over the Tsarina Elizabeth, but ended his life in exile in London.

53

the Tsarina to sign the treaty which His Majesty King George 'so earnestly desired'.

It is not known at what stage d'Eon abandoned his disguise, but he undoubtedly did, long before leaving St Petersburg. Far from being upset or annoyed by the deception, the Tsarina was even more delighted to discover he was a man. He was offered a government post and high rank in the Imperial Russian Army, and declined with such tact and grace that the old lady gave him a jewelled snuff-box in token of her affection. As a spy and diplomat, d'Eon had been an outstanding success, and when recalled to Paris Louis XV provided him with an annual salary of 3,000 livres and a permanent post as his personal representative.

D'Eon was sent off on a number of intelligence and diplomatic missions, sometimes as himself and sometimes as the irresistible Mademoiselle de Beaumont. When Louis XV and George II at length declared war on each other in 1756 (The Seven Years' War), d'Eon became aide-de-camp to the Duke de Broglie, who was in charge of the French intelligence service. It was somewhat of a surprise to d'Eon's military colleagues that anyone who could apparently slip so easily into the clothes and character of a girl could also be an intrepid soldier. His chief exploit on active service was to restore a dangerous situation by bringing up ammunition wagons under intense enemy artillery fire.

His career in France came to an end when he aroused the jealousy of Madame de Pompadour by becoming too close a confidant of the King. He escaped to England, taking with him, as a sensible precaution against future unpleasantness or poverty, a collection of letters written by Louis XV. These documents revealed the duplicity underlying 'peace' moves being made by Louis XV and his minister Choiseul, and d'Eon, spy, diplomat, soldier and female impersonator, now turned blackmailer. The French court made prolonged efforts to discredit and dispose of him, using propaganda and poison, but the intelligent and agile Chevalier was more than a match for his enemies – who seemed to try everything. On one occasion, hearing peculiar moans and cries in the wall of his lodgings, d'Eon thrust his rapier up the chimney and brought down a sweep, who admitted he had been hired by the French ambassador to 'haunt' the building. The idea was that d'Eon would complain, nothing would be found, and his enemies would arrange for him to be certified as insane. Incarceration was then the only 'cure' for madness.

Eventually d'Eon dictated his own financial terms for the surrender of the letters – some of which had been published from time to time to stimulate interest – but Louis XV died during the negotiations. His successor, Louis XVI, appreciated d'Eon's ability to make serious trouble between France and England, and a settlement was finally reached in 1775. D'Eon died in England in 1810, at the age of eighty-two; a strange, talented and lonely man.

CHAPTER SIX

In America and France

While the Chevalier d'Eon was successfully preventing George II from hiring Russian mercenaries to protect Hanover against the designs of Louis XV, the French in North America were putting into effect their plan to enclose the British Colonies by occupying the Ohio valley and blocking any westward expansion. This led to the French and Indian War, which really began with the skirmish on the Youghiogheny river on 28 May 1754, between a force led by George Washington, the twenty-one-year-old Adjutant General of the Virginia Militia, and a detachment from the French garrison of Fort Duquesne (later Pittsburgh). Perhaps it was on this expedition – to collect information on the French incursions – that Washington first developed his interest in intelligence which was to be of considerable advantage in his struggle against the British. He won his first action against the French, but was forced to surrender a few days afterwards when the rest of the garrison from Fort Duquesne besieged him, and took revenge at Fort Necessity.

From the intelligence point of view, the main features of the long war in North America, which ended on 7 September 1760 with Governor Vaudreuil's capitulation to General Jeffrey Amherst at Montreal, were Wolfe's solution to the problem of Quebec and the efficiency of Amherst's intelligence organization.

There are several different stories of how Wolfe learned of the steep path up the Heights of Abraham; what was so unusual was his 'security', in that no one but he knew where the landing was to take

The taking of Quebec, 1759. Wolfe's extreme 'security-mindedness', most unusual for the time, was entirely justified but did not endear him to his officers.

place. A few hours before the night operation began, his three Brigadier-Generals, Townshend, Monckton and Murray, wrote a joint letter 'begging leave to request distinct orders as to the place, or plans, we are to attack'. Wolfe, never very popular with his officers, sent the crushing reply: 'It is not the usual thing to point out in public orders the direct spot of an attack, nor for an inferior officer not charged with a particular duty, to ask instructions on that point.'

Wolfe's attitude was probably justified. Operational plans were often discussed openly, and prisoners of war and deserters were wont to give all the information they possessed because they were not trained to do otherwise. Yet excessive secrecy can render intelligence ineffective, and too tight a control over essential information can make things very awkward for a subordinate if anything happens to his commander.

General Jeffrey (later Lord) Amherst had a thorough understanding of military intelligence. His operations were therefore invariably successful but, because he achieved all his objectives without a major battle and the loss of thousands of men, his quality, on a level with Marl-

General Jeffrey Amherst (1717–97), conqueror of Canada, had such a fine grasp of military intelligence that his aims were all achieved without major battles.

borough and Wellington, has seldom been acknowledged. He too knew the importance of security. 'I kept my operations secret,' he wrote in his journal (16 May 1759). 'If the Indians know them the French will have it; though ever so much an Indian friend, it is their business to give intelligence on both sides.' His journal makes fascinating reading for the insight it gives into the methods of an expert military 'spymaster', and the mechanics of collection, collation and interpretation in converting into intelligence the information obtained from spies, deserters, prisoners of war and captured enemy documents.

One of the unfortunate effects of the English victory in the French and Indian War (the North American campaigns of the Seven Years' War) was to remove the threat of French aggression, and this, though not recognized at the time, was the only link binding the Colonies in America to the English crown. So when George III's minister George Grenville tried to shift some of the burden of expense for defending the Colonies onto the Colonies themselves, the Americans did not feel they were under any pressure to co-operate. Rebellion was in the air long before the so-called Boston Massacre in March 1770, or the shooting on the village green at Lexington in April 1775. Knowing the French would be eager to avenge their global defeat in the Seven Years' War, the Americans sent one of their most prominent citizens, Benjamin Franklin, who also happened to be a scientist and inventor of international repute, to be their diplomatic representative in Paris.

Even the most sensible men, cautious and wary by nature, are, from the spymaster's point of view, vulnerable through their own particular subject. Their defences tend to crumble under the influence of someone they feel as a kindred soul, who genuinely shares their interest; and so, when a Dr Edward Bancroft, also a scientist of some distinction, and quoted as being 'gentle and kindly', was introduced to Benjamin Franklin, it is not surprising that the two men should have become friends. Bancroft undoubtedly had a great admiration for Franklin's superior intellect and was charmed by his engaging personality, but he had been sent to Franklin's embassy at Passy, in Paris, with a definite job to do.

During practically the whole of the War of American Independence, from 1776 until the surrender of General Lord Cornwallis at Yorktown in October 1781, Bancroft supplied Lord Wentworth at the British Foreign Office with far more detailed information of America's international relations and foreign policy than ever reached either the Second Continental Congress or the American Commander-in-Chief, George Washington.

George III, who took a great personal interest in espionage, for a time gave every encouragement to Bancroft, who thoroughly enjoyed being a spy. By nature he was a gambler, thriving on risk spiced with danger, and it was gambling that got him into trouble in the end. He began to speculate in securities connected with the American Colonies, and when the King heard of this he immediately assumed Bancroft was a double agent. In a sense, he was. For years he had been supplying

Benjamin Franklin (1706–90), scientist, inventor and American diplomatic representative in Paris. His enthusiasm for science blinded him to the possibility that a fellow scientist could also be a British spy.

Franklin with documents and information collected on his frequent trips to London, but the real object of these visits to the court of St James had been to report on the Americans. When he returned to Paris he took with him carefully prepared material provided by his English spymasters. The King, obstinate and autocratic, dismissed him, though Lord Wentworth surreptitiously arranged for him to receive a pension for his valuable services. When Franklin was told what Bancroft had been doing, he refused to believe it. But Bancroft's efforts do not seem to have had any effect on Franklin's mission, because he obtained from the French the supplies, money and naval and military aid the American Colonists needed so badly.

The war itself, being in the nature of a domestic quarrel, invited espionage on the largest scale, yet intelligence systems developed slowly and remained small. The British and their Hessian mercenaries never had any proper organization, and the spies they did use were not very capable. A certain Lieutenant Nathan Palmer was discovered in the camp of that tough old Connecticut farmer and innkeeper General Israel Putnam, who hanged him immediately after a brief trial, and the fate of another Nathan was similar – the famous American Nathan Hale, who was captured while in disguise and carrying incriminating papers. Hale was hanged by the British in 1776, and made sure of his place in American history with his remark, 'I regret that I have but one life to give for my country.'

Nathan Hale, hero of the American Revolution, is shown penetrating the British camp disguised as a Dutch schoolmaster. His nervousness led to a search which disclosed documents hidden in his shoes. He was hanged in 1776.

General George Washington, commanding the 'rebel' Continental Army, seems to have been far more 'intelligence-conscious' than any of his British opponents. Between 1775 and 1781 he spent a total of 17,617 dollars – scrupulously accounted for – on espionage. He had learned much from his earlier experience of active service against the French, especially when he was General Edward Braddock's staff officer on the expedition to Fort Duquesne which ended with the disastrous battle on the Monongahela river.

Yet it was not until August 1777 that he set up the first American intelligence organization, operated by an officer named Major Benjamin Tallmadge of the Connecticut cavalry regiment of Sheldon's Dragoons, who had graduated from Yale University at the same time as Nathan Hale. Tallmadge was instructed to recruit and train agents for missions behind the British lines. In particular, he was to penetrate the headquarters of General Sir William Howe, and concentrate his main effort on General Sir Henry Clinton's military base at New York.

Though not a spymaster himself, Washington knew how to direct an intelligence service and how to train his intelligence officers. He preferred to deal only with Tallmadge and not with Tallmadge's agents, thus observing the principle of keeping intelligence under centralized control. On one occasion Tallmadge sent him a report on what appeared to be a blank sheet of paper. In fact he had used a secret ink, known as a 'sympathetic stain', first suggested by James Jay, an American in Benjamin Franklin's delegation in Paris, and brought to America by the Marquis de Lafayette, one of the best known of the French 'volunteers' sent by Louis XVI to aid the 'rebels'. Disconcerted by such an obvious blunder, Washington told Tallmadge never to do that sort of thing again; it was bound to arouse suspicion and it was quite probable that the British had the reagent.

'A much better way', he wrote, 'is to send a letter in the Tory [Loyalist] style, with some mixture of family matters, and between the lines in the remaining part of the sheet, communicate with the stain the intended intelligence.'

Tallmadge learned from his early mistakes, and he built up an effective organization based on Walsingham's principle that the right man in the right place is worth more than a host of freelance agents. A great deal of useful information on Howe's headquarters in Philadelphia was obtained by Mrs Lydia Darragh, who lived directly opposite in the same street, and she was largely responsible for the British defeat at Whitemarsh in December 1777. What became known as the Culper Ring operated in New York, where one of Tallmadge's most valuable spies – even though subsequently suspected of being a double agent – was Thomas Rivington, editor and printer of the Loyalist *New York Gazette*. His anti-rebel propaganda provided excellent cover for his loyalty to Tallmadge, and his intelligence reports were concealed in carefully re-bound copies of school textbooks. Another such agent was Robert Townsend, a contemporary of Tallmadge and Nathan Hale at Yale. He kept a store in New York which came to be used by the

British as a meeting-place where any subject could be freely discussed – and was.

The information he obtained was passed to a courier named Austin Roe, a man with a passion for horses and riding, known to be restless and always on the move. Many of his journeys took him to Setauket where he passed the time of day with an old friend, Abraham Woodhull. Oddly enough, Roe's visits seemed to make Woodhull fidgety for, soon after, he would ride north and (an echo of Rahab's scarlet thread) would look for a clothes-line in a back yard at a certain place on the Long Island shore. If a black petticoat and white handkerchiefs had been pegged out to dry, he would know that Caleb Brewster was ready. Brewster, a boatman who spent a lot of his time fishing in Long Island Sound at all hours of the day and night, delivered the despatches to Tallmadge at a prearranged spot on the Connecticut coast.

This well organized system obtained a great deal of information from New York, the British main headquarters from August 1776 until November 1783, and was never seriously compromised during all the time it was in operation. In fact it was not for nearly 100 years that the cover names of Samuel Culper Senior and Junior – for Woodhull and Townsend respectively – and that of Mr John Bolton for Tallmadge, were identified.

On the other hand, the British seem to have relied overmuch on 'casual' sources, in other words, being able to pick up information from Loyalists, disaffected rebels, and anyone else who might volunteer it. They certainly had a few spies, such as Dr Benjamin Church of Philadelphia and Benjamin Thompson, who used codes and invisible inks to pass details of American forces, morale and plans to the British General Gage, but the capture and execution of Nathan Palmer, a regular army officer, discouraged recruitment among Loyalists as well as other soldiers. Naturally enough, the British tended to be sceptical of information offered to them by Colonists – it was not easy to judge who was a friend and who was an enemy. One of the worst examples of ignoring a source occurred at Trenton, where Washington, acting on information supplied by John Honeyman, weaver and butcher of Griggstown, New Jersey, saved the cause of the Revolution. With a force of 2,400 men he crossed the Delaware river on Christmas night, 1776, took the Trenton garrison of 1,300 Hessians, commanded by Colonel Rahl, completely by surprise, and routed it. 1,000 of Rahl's men were taken prisoner, and the commander himself was mortally wounded. Found in one of his pockets was an unopened letter from a Loyalist giving full information of the proposed attack.

A great deal has been written about Major John André of the 54th Foot, Sir Henry Clinton's Adjutant General in New York, who was hanged as a spy at Tappan on 2 October 1780; but in fact he was only a courier and 'negotiator' acting as the link-man between Clinton and the notorious American traitor Benedict Arnold who, ironically enough, was by far the best soldier of all the military commanders on either side.

The last journey of a courier. The British Major John André, link between the traitor Arnold and the British forces, died because he regarded espionage merely as an exciting game.

Arnold, furious at being passed over for promotion, largely because of somewhat indiscreet appropriations of public money, and also heavily in debt, offered to sell West Point, the key to the Hudson river, to the British for £20,000. André, dressed in civilian clothes and with his boots stuffed with papers giving full details of the American defences, was stopped by a small American patrol on the post road to Tarrytown. Although provided with a pass signed by Arnold which made him out to be 'John Anderson. Merchant', he blurted out to his captors that he was a British officer, and offered them 100 guineas to let him go. Escorted to the gallows by Major Benjamin Tallmadge, he died just as bravely as Nathan Hale.

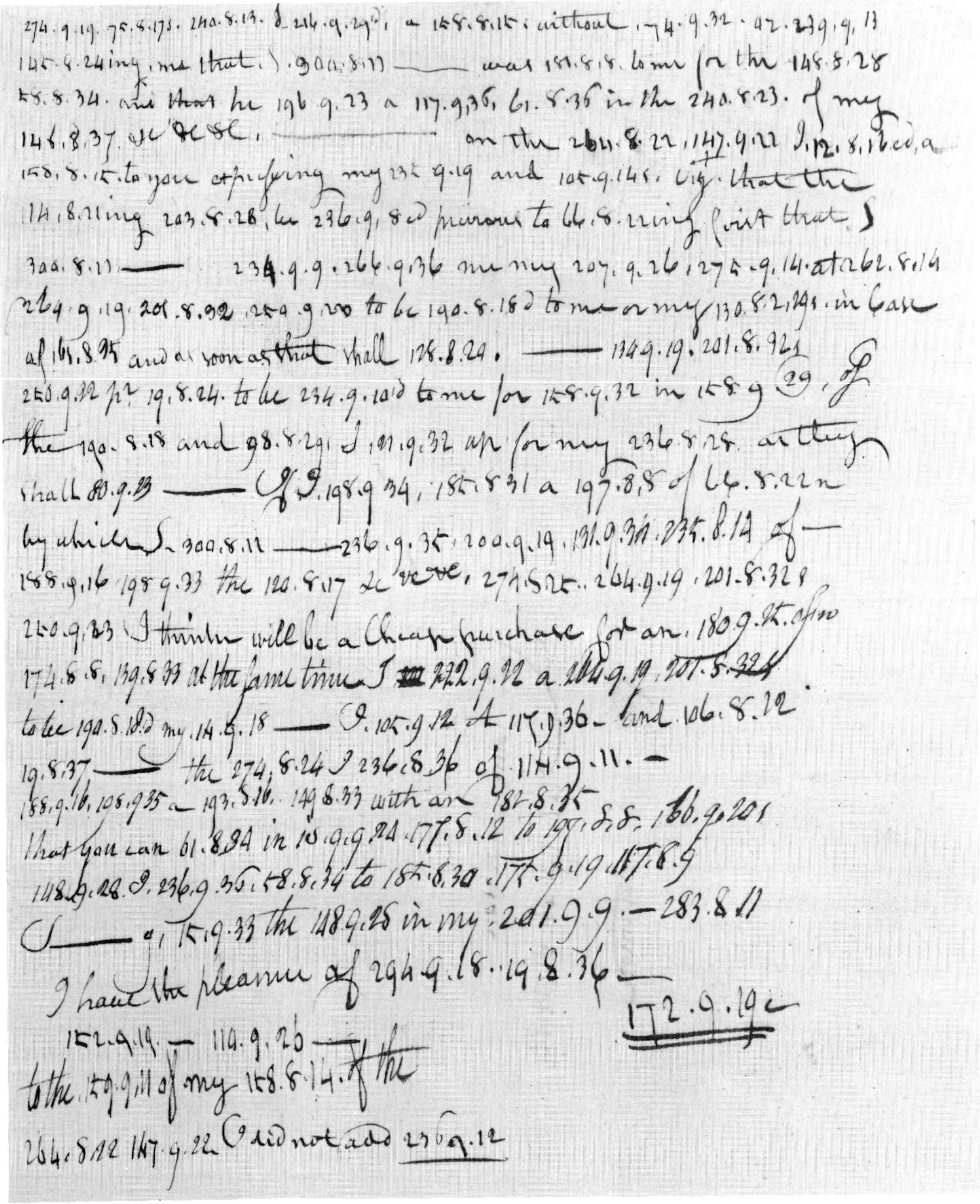

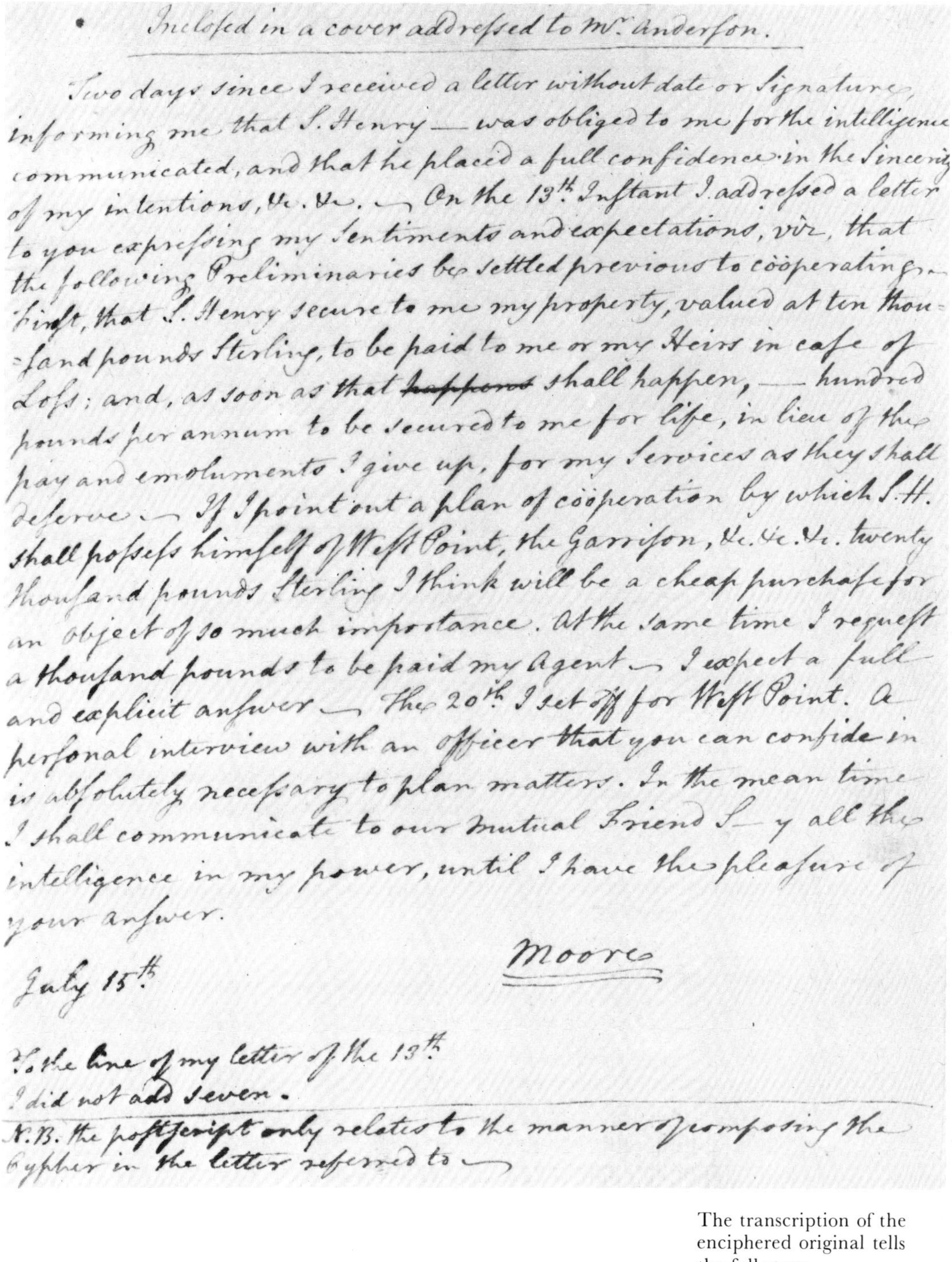

Inclosed in a cover addressed to Mr. Anderson.

Two days since I received a letter without date or Signature, informing me that S. Henry — was obliged to me for the intelligence communicated, and that he placed a full confidence in the Sincerity of my intentions, &c. &c. — On the 13th Instant I addressed a letter to you expressing my Sentiments and expectations, viz, that the following Preliminaries be settled previous to coöperating. First, that S. Henry secure to me my property, valued at ten thousand pounds Sterling, to be paid to me or my Heirs in case of Loss; and, as soon as that ~~happens~~ shall happen, — hundred pounds per annum to be secured to me for life, in lieu of the pay and emoluments I give up, for my Services as they shall deserve. — If I point out a plan of coöperation by which S. H. shall possess himself of West Point, the Garrison, &c. &c. &c. twenty thousand pounds Sterling I think will be a cheap purchase for an object of so much importance. At the same time I request a thousand pounds to be paid my Agent. — I expect a full and explicit answer. — The 20th I set off for West Point. A personal interview with an officer that you can confide in is absolutely necessary to plan matters. In the mean time I shall communicate to our Mutual Friend S——y all the intelligence in my power, until I have the pleasure of your answer.

                             Moore

July 15th

To the line of my letter of the 13th
I did not add seven. —

N.B. the postscript only relates to the manner of composing the
Cypher in the letter referred to —

The transcription of the enciphered original tells the full story.

It has been said that Washington refused a reprieve because the British had hanged Nathan Hale, but Washington, a man of great moral as well as physical stature, was incapable of sending a man to his death for such a reason. In any case, André brought most of his troubles upon himself. He had been specifically ordered by Clinton not to go behind the American lines and in no circumstances to take off his uniform. He did both. However, his fate did at least serve the useful purpose of emphasizing the essential differences between an intelligence officer and a spy, and of providing a sharp warning to all soldiers who, given a military intelligence task, might be tempted to play the spy.

André's example may have had an effect in the British army as a whole because, nearly thirty years later, Wellington's intelligence officers took care not to repeat André's mistakes. None of them, except Captain John Grant, who never tried to be anything but a spy, would have considered adopting a disguise. They performed their duties wearing the uniform of their regiments, often riding deep into enemy-held country, secure in the knowledge that if captured they would be – or ought to be – treated as prisoners of war and not hanged as spies.

While the war went on in America, and while Dr Bancroft continued to delude Benjamin Franklin in Passy, several attempts were made by the French and the Americans to sabotage the British war effort. Though fires were started – and soon extinguished – in Portsmouth and Bristol dockyards, the agents sent over from France or recruited in England were strikingly incompetent. The best known of them, a man called Jack the Painter whose real name was James Hill, achieved some notoriety. His odd behaviour attracted suspicion from the moment he arrived at a Portsmouth inn during December 1776. When drunk he boasted of his espionage activities, and managed to set his room on fire while experimenting with an incendiary device. Naturally, when a fire broke out in a rope yard at the docks, no time was wasted in arresting the obvious culprit. He was hanged as a spy and saboteur at the dockyard gate on 10 April 1777.

When America had won her independence the British troops returned to England, many of the Hessian mercenaries became American citizens, and all the French troops who did not follow their example went back to France filled with new ideas about life, liberty and the pursuit of happiness which were not at all welcome to the *ancien régime*. A combination of these ideas, economic chaos, and the failure of harvests, led to the French Revolution which, in due course, followed the pattern of most so-called democratic rebellions by throwing up a dictator more absolute than the original system of government destroyed by the revolution. Revolution offers special advantages for self-promotion and the settling of old scores, and creates its own atmosphere of malice and deceit, so it is not remarkable that in France it produced a number of unattractive characters.

One of the most notorious was Héron, the double agent spying *for* the Committee of Public Safety *on* the Committee of General Security, and vice versa. He suffered from a persecution mania and was convinced that everyone was spying on him, though he seems to have been, initially, in a strong position. 'The names are called over,' he said, 'the heads fall and pouf! pouf! The thing is done!' Defended as 'indispensable' by the Public Prosecutor, the infamous Fouquier-Tinville, and by Robespierre himself, Héron ran a spy and informer organization which became an integral part of the Terror that in due course destroyed him.

Perhaps the most extraordinary personality during the period of *le grand Peur* (1789–90) and that of the Terror (1793–4) was a fanatical Royalist and anti-revolutionary, the Gascon Baron Jean de Batz. Born in 1761, commissioned into the Queen's Dragoons as a cornet in 1776, and appointed Deputy in the States General in 1789, he was a man in the tradition of the Musketeers of Dumas, larger than life and apparently under the special protection of Providence. His aim was to promote the Terror by feeding the guillotine with denounced revolutionaries to the point where the guillotine itself destroyed the Revolution – and he seems to have succeeded. It is almost incredible that in the Paris of the Terror he not only survived but organized and controlled a *Royalist* network of espionage and informers which functioned capably. Indirectly and unintentionally he paved the way for the Corsican artilleryman, Napoleon Bonaparte, to become for a time the Emperor of France and the master of continental Europe.

Two of the most prominent names in the story of intelligence in France are those of Joseph Fouché and Karl Schulmeister. Fouché, born in Nantes in May 1758, was destined for the Church. In 1779 he adopted the robe and tonsure of the Oratorian Order but, always reluctant to commit himself, for ten years refused to take vows or be ordained. In 1792, at the age of thirty-four, he suddenly abandoned his clerical garb and was elected to the National Convention by the citizens of Nantes. His public career had begun. During the next two decades, in bewildering succession, he was to be first a conservative and then a radical politician; revolutionary, republican and Jacobin; for Bonaparte and against him; supporter of the Napoleonic empire and minister to the restored Bourbon monarchy. He rose to the heights of Minister of Police, millionaire and Duke of Otranto, yet of all things he was first and foremost a spymaster, lurking in the shadows beside the net of espionage which had been flung across the country by his secret police.

Conscious that Fouché was becoming too powerful, Napoleon dismissed him in 1802, only to reinstate him two years later when he realized that the internal security situation in his empire warranted a man of peculiar talents. Although suspected, rightly, of subversion and conspiracy, Fouché remained at the head of the police for another six years before being again dismissed in 1810. His place was taken by General René Savary, Duke of Rovigno, who rapidly made himself even more disliked throughout France than the man he had succeeded, but his chief claim to notoriety is that he recognized the talents of Karl Schulmeister, and recruited him to the ranks of espionage.

Joseph Fouché (1763–1820), a classic example of the spymaster whose organization is primarily designed to serve himself.

Fouché and Savary were, pre-eminently, 'civilian' spymasters in that their objectives, when not actively personal, were political. Schulmeister was a military spy – of outstanding ability. His skill, courage and resourcefulness were of the highest standard, and his loyalty to the Emperor Napoleon was constant. Like so many spies of this type, in the end his qualities were ill rewarded.

Son of a Lutheran minister, Karl Schulmeister was born in Alsace on 5 August 1770, and as a youth his income came ostensibly from a small grocery-cum-hardware shop, but in fact from smuggling: at the age of seventeen he was describing himself as a professional *contrebandier*. His first contact with Savary, then a colonel, was in 1799, but it was not until 1804 that he was recruited as a secret agent in connection with the abduction, and subsequent execution in the dry moat at Vincennes, of Louis de Bourbon, Duke d'Enghien. Schulmeister's main part in the plot was that of forger; he is said to have written the letter, purporting to be from a girl well known to d'Enghien, which lured the unfortunate man from the safety of Baden-Baden to the place where he was kidnapped by Savary's agents. Savary paid Schulmeister the equivalent of £5,000 for his services in disposing of the Emperor's 'enemy'.

Karl Schulmeister, whose espionage work for Napoleon led to the defeat of the Austrian forces at Ulm and Austerlitz. His part in the capture of the Duke d'Enghien (*below*) was his first important coup as a spy.

In the following year, 1805, Savary introduced his protégé to Napoleon with the remark, 'Here, sir, is a man all brains and no heart.' Napoleon was interested, and said so. Schulmeister welcomed this contact with the Emperor because he had two great ambitions which only Napoleon could satisfy: elevation to a dukedom and the ribbon of the Legion of Honour. At this stage he did not know that the Corsican dictator held definite views about spies: one, that 'the spy is a natural traitor', and the other, 'for a spy, gold is the only suitable reward'.

Later on that year there was an urgent need for a reliable French agent to be placed in the headquarters of the Austrian commander Marshal Mack von Leiberich. Knowing Mack was an ardent Royalist who was unable to believe that France was loyal to a Corsican upstart, Napoleon briefed Schulmeister for a task which the spy, with his pretensions to the aristocracy, found particularly attractive.

In due course, Mack received a letter apparently signed by a young Hungarian nobleman living in France, who complained bitterly that he was being banished by Napoleon on suspicion of being an Austrian spy. Protesting his innocence, he offered to serve Austria in any capacity, and indicated that he had valuable sources of information, especially on the dissension and dissatisfaction in France, available to him in Paris. This was perfectly true; the principal source was Napoleon himself, who provided material for Schulmeister to use in winning Mack's confidence. Evidence of noble Hungarian ancestry was provided by Schulmeister himself, again employing his skill as a forger. Within a few months the Alsatian spy had not only been given a commission in the Austrian army but had actually been appointed Head of Military Intelligence. Furthermore, with the help of Napoleon's gold, he had recruited two Austrian officers, Majors Rulski and Wend, whose task was to confirm his intelligence reports to Marshal Mack.

One of the results of this rapid promotion was the virtual destruction of the Austrian army, first at Ulm and then at Austerlitz. Napoleon was undoubtedly a brilliant strategist, unsurpassed in his skill in the deployment of forces for battle, but his reliance upon accurate and timely intelligence is seldom given the emphasis it merits.

Triumphant, elated by his own bravery and skill in deception, Schulmeister greeted his master at the gates of Vienna. His boasting infuriated the French, while the Austrians swore they would be avenged. He was rewarded with huge sums of money but no dukedom and no decoration – despite the fact that the abominable Fouché was made a duke.

Then, somewhat out of keeping with the mentality of a spy (although the Chevalier d'Eon had set a precedent) Schulmeister vindicated all his boastfulness by applying for, and being granted, a cavalry command in the French army. He led a charge at Landshut which scattered the rearguard of the Austrian General Baron Johann Hiller; his attack on the Russian guns at Friedland left deep shrapnel scars on his face as a lasting reminder; and when he was subsequently sent to investigate

Schulmeister's mansion, built from the proceeds of his espionage career. The Austrians assigned an entire artillery regiment to its demolition.

civil disturbances at Strasbourg he confronted the ringleader at the head of an angry crowd, and immediately shot him dead with one ball from his pistol.

Having done so much to bring about the defeat of Austria, Schulmeister lost all influence after Napoleon's second marriage, to the Austrian Archduchess Marie Louise, in 1810. Not surprisingly, her resentment of his former activities forced him to retire to the huge estate he had bought in Alsace.

The tide of Napoleonic, and French, fortunes turned at Leipzig – the Battle of the Nations, in October 1813. Fighting a magnificent defensive campaign, Napoleon fell back on Paris. The Austrians stormed through Alsace and took the trouble to detach a whole regiment of artillery to destroy the stately home Schulmeister had built with the profits of espionage and deception. He escaped. He rejoined the Emperor when he came back from Elba but, arrested after the disaster of Waterloo, was able to save himself only by payment of an enormous ransom. In trying to retrieve his fortunes he gambled on the Bourse and lost everything, except, strangely enough, the goodwill of his Alsatian neighbours. No doubt they recalled his services to them as a smuggler of luxuries they could not otherwise have obtained.

He lived for nearly forty more years, not unhappily, as the proprietor of a small tobacconist's shop in Strasbourg, and the year of his eightieth birthday was made memorable by the visit to his shop of Napoleon III, who recalled Schulmeister's services to his imperial uncle. He died in poverty in 1853, and was buried in the cemetery of St Urban in Strasbourg.

CHAPTER SEVEN
The Peninsula and Waterloo

Although England's first prime minister, Sir Robert Walpole – in office from 1721 to 1742 – shared Defoe's views on intelligence, and said it should be developed to the stage where no gun could be fired in Europe without England knowing why, his immediate successors did little to pursue his ideal. Even when William Pitt (later Lord Chatham) rescued his country from the disasters of the Duke of Newcastle's administration, and in 1757 took over the running of the Seven Years' War, the spies, agents and informants in touch with European affairs still lacked proper direction and centralized control.

When all the major and most of the minor states of Europe formed the League of Armed Neutrality at the time when Britain was losing the war against her American Colonies, the government in London was taken by surprise, as so often before. Many of the old intelligence lessons had been learned again in America, yet the prejudice persisted. To many of the British and Americans involved in the war there was still something despicable about espionage.

Neither in Britain nor America was there any attempt to set up any sort of permanent intelligence organization, and no effort was made to increase the scope of collection beyond the normal functions of diplomats in the international political field and of scouts and patrols in military operations. Britain and America had no counterpart to men like Fouché, Savary and Schulmeister. So, after ten years of uneasy peace following the loss of the American Colonies, the French declaration of war against Britain in 1793 came as another surprise.

Frederick Duke of York was required to undertake a campaign in Flanders without any trained staff, without any intelligence or administrative services, and without any help from the politicians who gave him his orders. Defeat and evacuation from the continent were inevitable. England then had to muster her resources to resist invasion; an operation which Napoleon found to be rather more complicated than he had imagined. In order to secure a respite from active operations while he collected and trained his military and naval forces, he negotiated the Treaty of Amiens, signed in March 1802.

The 'peace' lasted only fourteen months – Pitt (the Younger) had to declare war again in May 1803 – but during that time English tourists flocked to France, mainly to see what was left of Paris after the

Revolution. Among them were spies interested in Napoleon's plans, and they brought back the information that there was a special *Bureau d'Intelligence* in the French war ministry, and that a select corps of 117 men, known as the *Guides-Interprètes de l'Armée d'Angleterre*, had been raised specially for intelligence purposes. This corps was part of the Army of the Coasts of the Ocean, 200,000 strong, now being deployed in camps along the Channel coast. All this made renewal of the war unavoidable, and it also led to the establishment of the Depot of Military Knowledge, on the top floor of the commander-in-chief's headquarters at Horse Guards in Whitehall. This 'Depot' was the embryo of the military intelligence staff and of the Survey Department. It was to consist of four separate branches dealing with the collection of information by overseas agents, mainly for contingency planning; the collection of information needed for troop movements anywhere in the world; the formation of a library as the basis for the study of past and current operations; and lastly, the collection, preparation and copying of maps.

Although the war started again only a few weeks after the Depot had been authorized, and before it could be fully manned, it remained in being. Many of the officers earmarked for it – like Lieutenant-Colonel George Murray of the 3rd Foot Guards – were posted to more active appointments. Unfortunately this new department, founded by

The Horse Guards, Whitehall. Intelligence found a constricted home in the attic of the commander-in-chief's headquarters.

Opposite, Guide Interprète de l'Armée d'Angleterre in Napoleon's intelligence corps, trained for duties in England after the anticipated French invasion and occupation.

the Duke of York, was inevitably affected by his resignation over the scandal involving his mistress, Mary Anne Clarke. Although so sensibly designed to meet vital needs, when the war ended it lost its motivation and for the next forty years made no significant contribution to military 'Knowledge'. Nevertheless, it was a beginning.

The concentration of French army corps along the coast westwards from Ostend to St Malo resulted, somewhat naturally, in the movement of a cloud of spies across the Channel, mostly, it appears, from England to the continent. Since Napoleon held the initiative and had already, in the pause following the Treaty of Amiens, collected most of the information he needed, the main intelligence effort was British – directed at finding out the place, the time and the strength of the invasion.

By September 1805 Napoleon had come to the conclusion that the British navy presented him with an insoluble problem. He marched his armies south, to Ulm, and the defeat of Austria. In the following month Nelson's victory at Trafalgar removed any further threat of invasion.

The succession of victories in eastern Europe, culminating in the Treaty of Tilsit in 1807, made Napoleon master of the continent. He had the greatest contempt for the army of the nation of shopkeepers and believed that in time Britain would have to come to terms. In the meantime there was no point in wasting men and money on espionage in England, and Fouché's organization could take care of any hostile spies in France – but Fouché did not find out about Mr Macpherson, a Highlander who took care to conceal his activities and opinions. .

As a young man, Macpherson had taken up the cause of the Young Pretender, Bonnie Prince Charlie, and after the destruction of Jacobite hopes at Culloden in April 1746, he had fled to France, for centuries a sanctuary for the Scottish enemies of England. He set himself up as a jeweller in Paris, quietly earned his living, and did not concern himself with politics. Years later, during the Terror, he was suddenly arrested as an enemy of the Revolution, imprisoned in the Conciergerie and sentenced to death. He was lucky. His name was a long way down the list and, before the tumbril came for him, Robespierre's head had fallen into Sanson's basket. Since Robespierre had ordered his arrest, Macpherson was now released. He reopened his shop and very soon afterwards moved silently into the world of espionage, presumably in the cause of the French Royalists, as there is no reason to suppose he had changed his view about England. He was soon an influential member of the spy ring which was probably run by de Batz. It was centred on Paris and had agents inside Fouché's police department and in the War Office – Clarke, the Duke de Feltre, was Minister for War. Many of the spies and couriers in this ring were priests and lay members of the Church who, ever since the nationalization of hereditary Church lands and the reduction of the French clergy to the status of poorly paid servants of the State (in the 'reforms' of 1789), had felt no loyalty towards the Revolution or the imperial court which succeeded it. Subsequently Macpherson became linked with British military intelligence through the network of Roman Catholic clergy, the university of Salamanca and the elderly Irish secret agent and university professor, Doctor Curtis.

Once again, as so often before, the black-robed priests, ostensibly employed on parochial duties and therefore arousing no suspicion, took part in affairs far removed from their pastoral responsibilities.

Napoleon took what he thought were adequate steps to deny the British a foothold on the continent, but his mishandling of the situation in Spain, when he lured the Spanish King Charles VI and his son Ferdinand to Bayonne, forced Charles to abdicate, and then put his own brother Joseph Bonaparte on the throne in Madrid, prompted the Spaniards to appeal for help from their ancient enemies the English. Sir Arthur Wellesley, whom Napoleon scornfully nicknamed the 'Sepoy General' in token of his service in India, landed with an army of 30,000 men at the mouth of the Mondego river in July 1808.

Wellesley's victorious campaigns in southern India had been models of their kind because he took pains to study his enemy and was not satisfied with merely finding out where and how strong they were. To him, the character of the commanders, the spirit of the troops, their training, battle experience and administrative support were equally important, and on a par with such things as topography and climate. He knew what effect a hitherto unseen sunken road could have on a cavalry charge; he had seen how a thunderstorm could suddenly turn a dry watercourse into an unfordable obstacle.

Appointed to command the expeditionary force in the Iberian peninsula, he sent ahead of him a military mission consisting of officers specially briefed to collect information not only on the French armies of occupation but on the military resources of the Spanish and Portuguese, and the terrain. In England, little was known about Spain or Portugal. Very few Englishmen could speak either language, and there were practically no maps. In these circumstances the landing of a comparatively small army on the unknown coast of enemy-held country was, by any standard, a risky enterprise. It was a measure of Wellesley's generalship that within five weeks of that landing he had defeated the French General Junot twice, at the battles of Roliça and Vimiero – and as a result, Junot never received his marshal's baton.

Superseded by two elderly and incapable senior officers, Sir Harry Burrard and Sir Hew Dalrymple, immediately after Vimiero, Wellesley was prevented from following up and annihilating Junot's army. Worse still, his name became associated with the shameful Convention of Cintra which allowed the defeated French to return to France, in British warships, and prepare to fight again. Sir John Moore, appointed to command when Burrard, Dalrymple and Wellesley were recalled to England, advanced on Madrid.

He was fortunate in that one of the intelligence officers chosen by Wellesley, Captain John Waters, intercepted a despatch which gave details of Napoleon's plan to encircle the British force. The retreat to

Arthur Wellesley, Duke of Wellington. 'All the business of war', he wrote, '...is to endeavour to find out what you don't know by what you do.'

Corunna in January 1808 was followed by the battle against Marshal Soult, Moore's death in action, and the evacuation of his army. Three months later Wellesley, restored to high command, returned with an army which forced Soult to flee from Oporto and, on 28 July 1809, defeated Marshal Victor at Talavera. Sir Arthur Wellesley became Viscount Wellington.

He had no illusions about the magnitude of his task: to drive the French armies out of Portugal and Spain with a British force seldom larger than a French army corps, and with whatever Portuguese and Spanish troops, regular or irregular, could be persuaded to support him.

Since he was always to be outnumbered and seldom entirely sure of his allies, Wellington relied upon intelligence, the one asset which could compensate for such disadvantages. In following the examples of Marlborough and Amherst he developed, for the first time, an organized system of military intelligence staffed by field intelligence officers who controlled sources and agencies recruited in the theatre of operations. He was his own head of intelligence, and of the men he chose for his intelligence staff he said, 'No army in the world ever produced the like.'

Initially, their principal duty was reconnaissance. This included getting to know the country and its inhabitants, the state of the roads, which rivers were navigable and where they could be crossed, likely routes the French would use in their operations, and so on. These officers worked under the direction of his Quartermaster-General, Sir George Murray (late of the Depot of Military Knowledge in Whitehall), whose main function was 'to regulate the marching, encamping and quartering of troops'. Movement orders could not be written without knowledge of the country, embracing such things as suitable camp sites, water supplies and the availability of provisions and forage. Above all, there was an urgent need for accurate maps.

The 'exploring officers', as they were called, were chosen on merit from cavalry regiments and infantry regiments of the line, and by the winter of 1810 most of central Portugal and a large area within Spain had been accurately mapped on the scale of four miles to the inch – by men on horseback. A mass of valuable topographical intelligence had been collected and recorded.

As time passed, these officers became separated into two categories: those mainly employed on survey and map-making, who acquired and reported information about the enemy as and when the opportunity arose, and those primarily interested in enemy activity, who included topographical information in their intelligence reports. In many cases it would be difficult to determine in which category a particular officer belonged, for the system operated by Murray and Wellington was extremely flexible, and all the exploring officers had a number of basic skills in common. They were all fine horsemen, highly mobile in difficult country; they were linguists, able to dispense with interpreters in collecting information from local inhabitants. They could express

Part of a map of Spain,
surveyed and drawn by
Wellington's 'exploring
officers'. This accurate
mapping operation,
carried out under difficult
conditions, contributed
greatly to British success
in the Peninsula.

EXPLANATION.

Sª. Sierra, Chain of mountains whose
peaks present the appearance of a Saw.

V. Valle, Valley.

Llano. Plain.

Peña, Rock.

Pta. Punta, Point.

Pto. Puerto, Harbour.

Nª. the names of Passes are in small
print, thus Guadarrama P.

C. Coll, a Defile.

R. Rio, River.

A. Arroyo, Rivulet.

Pte. Puente, Bridge.

Vª. Villa, Town.

F. Fuerte, Fort.

Vta. Venta, Inn.

—— de arriba, Upper.

—— de abaxo, Lower.

Calzada, Causeway.

Guadi an Arabic word which Signifies a river.

⊙ Cities.	○	Small Villages, Ventas &c.
✪ Fortified Towns.	▫	Forts.
⊙ Towns.	——	Principal Roads.
○ Principal Villages.		

A 'panorama' of
Pamplona drawn by
Andrew Leith Hay, one
of the famous quartet of
field intelligence officers
in the Peninsula.
Militarily, such a drawing
would be an invaluable
complement to a map.

Colonel George Scovell,
chief communications
officer and code-breaker.

themselves accurately and concisely on paper – the paper often being
small enough for concealment in the hollowed-out heel of a courier's
boot. They were extremely competent 'field sketchers', able to depict
landscapes, natural obstacles and enemy dispositions. Lastly, they were
all brave men.

Of those who dealt mainly with operational intelligence, the most
famous were Colquhoun Grant of the 11th Foot (Devons), Andrew
Leith Hay of the 29th Foot (Worcesters), John Waters of the 1st of
Foot (Royal Scots) and Charles Somers Cocks of the 16th Light
Dragoons. All were individualists, and their paths seldom crossed.

The efficiency and scope of the intelligence organization increased
rapidly, with the result that the flow of what Wellington called his
'secret correspondence' – the written and oral reports from sources and
agencies, intercepted enemy despatches and other captured documents – became too great for him to handle alone. Captain (later
Colonel) George Scovell, put in charge of communications in 1811,
became an expert at deciphering the operational codes used by the
French. It was he who broke the 'Great Paris Cipher'. Among the Scovell Papers now in the Public Record Office are masses of encoded
French documents transcribed in his neat hadwriting. Some of them
are torn, and dark stains indicate the fate of the unfortunate courier.

Wellington's system was designed to exploit all potential sources of
information. Broadly speaking, it can be divided into three principal
sections: first, the normal military sources, such as cavalry patrols and
troops on the move or in contact with the enemy, which provided either
the specific information a sub-unit had been tasked to obtain, or unsoli-
cited information of all kinds acquired by a unit on the march or from

local villagers at a camp site or billeting area. Secondly, many of his intelligence officers, particularly Colquhoun Grant, had their own networks mainly of *alcaldes* (mayors of towns and headmen of villages), priests, peasants and selected members of the Spanish guerrilla forces, who preyed on French outposts, cantonments and communications; and thirdly, the espionage agents, such as Captain John Grant, originally of the 4th Foot (The King's Own), and respectable citizens living in towns and cities garrisoned by the French. John Grant seems to have been a spy because he really enjoyed the excitement and danger – he had several narrow escapes from the French – and the respectable citizens were paid to send routine intelligence reports.

The *alcaldes* and priests produced all sorts of valuable material which enabled Wellington to build up an accurate enemy order of battle, but the priests were often under suspicion by the French. The really notable priest-spy was Dr Curtis, professor of astronomy and natural history at the university of Salamanca, and for many years Rector of the Irish College. Graduates from the university, dispersed throughout Portugal, Spain and France, and motivated by a shared hatred of the French, constituted a very large network of informants and couriers.

Lt-Col. Colquhoun Grant, Wellington's chief intelligence officer and the first officially appointed Head of the Intelligence Department in the field. Members of the local peasantry (*above*) proved valuable recruits for espionage networks organized by Grant and his colleagues.

77

The French Marshal Marmont had his suspicions of Dr Curtis at the time when Colquhoun Grant was captured near Sabugal in April 1812, and brought in to the French headquarters at Salamanca. Marmont believed, with good reason, that the venerable professor was passing information to Wellington on Grant's behalf and his own, and although nothing could be proved, Dr Curtis was expelled from the Irish College. His furniture and the valuable contents of his library were confiscated. Marmont went no further. Dr Curtis was a greatly respected member of Salamanca society and many of Marmont's own subordinates felt he had been harshly treated. The old Doctor himself was philosophical about his misfortune; he was probably well aware how lucky he had been to escape so lightly.

Colquhoun Grant was taken under strong escort to Bayonne where he was to be met by Fouché's thugs and probably murdered, but the letter making all the arrangements, written by Marmont's Chief of Staff, General de la Martinière, was intercepted by one of Colquhoun's friends, the guerrilla leader Julian Sanchez, whence it was delivered to Wellington and filed by George Scovell. Arriving at Bayonne, Grant escaped, with the connivance of French officers of his escort who admired his exploits, made contact with one of Dr Curtis's agents at Orleans, and was passed on into the care of Mr Macpherson in Paris. While in Paris, in the guise of an American officer, Colquhoun Grant was able to send messages overland to Wellington in Spain. After a series of extraordinary adventures he escaped to England and at length rejoined Wellington's headquarters at Lesaca.

Colquhoun Grant remained with Wellington until the fall of Toulouse and the end of hostilities in southwestern France in April 1814, and then went to the Staff College at Camberley. He was there when Napoleon landed at Golfe Juan, near Cannes, at the beginning of the Hundred Days. By this time most of Wellington's veteran troops, and many of the officers who had served under him in the Peninsula, were campaigning in America and trying, with some success, to burn down the White House in the new federal capital of Washington D.C. Officially appointed as the first Head of the Intelligence Department in the field, Grant was called to Brussels, where Wellington had formed his headquarters, but he spent very little time there before moving across the French frontier.

Napoleon had neglected to declare war before mobilizing his army, and so neither Wellington nor his Prussian ally Blücher quite knew what the situation was. They knew Napoleon would attack; they had good reason to believe he would make for Brussels, because in the past he had always aimed for enemy capitals; but they could not concentrate their forces until they knew the route, timings and strength of the French army. In the meantime, their forces had to watch a front of 130 miles, from Ostend in a great curve through Tournai and Mons to Liège.

It seems that Grant had gone into France to renew his contacts with Macpherson's spy ring, which had agents in the French War Office.

Opposite, intercepted by Spanish guerrillas, a letter from Marmont's Chief of Staff describes Colquhoun Grant's capture and recommends his delivery to the secret police (i.e. Fouché's assassins).

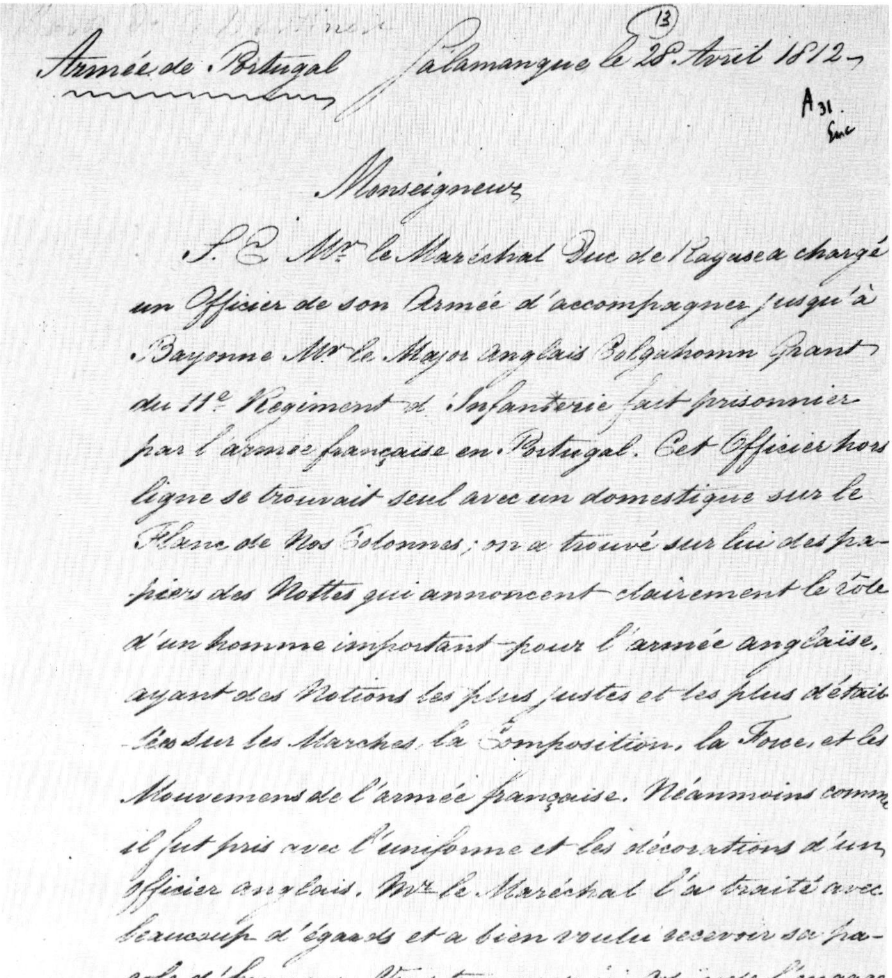

Armée de Portugal — Salamanque le 28 Avril 1812 — (13)

A 31
Ent

Monseigneur,

S. E. Mr. le Maréchal Duc de Raguse a chargé un Officier de son Armée d'accompagner jusqu'à Bayonne Mr. le Major anglais Belgrahonn Grant du 11e Regiment d'Infanterie fait prisonnier par l'armée française en Portugal. Cet Officier hors ligne se trouvait seul avec un domestique sur le Flanc de Nos Colonnes; on a trouvé sur lui des papiers des Notes qui annoncent clairement le rôle d'un homme important pour l'armée anglaise, ayant des Notions les plus justes et les plus détaillées sur les Marches, la Composition, la Force, et les Mouvemens de l'armée française. Néanmoins comme il fut pris avec l'uniforme et les décorations d'un Officier anglais, Mr. le Maréchal l'a traité avec beaucoup d'égards et a bien voulu recevoir sa parole d'honneur. Vous trouverez ici copie de l'engagement qu'il a contracté. Mais son Excellence croit qu'il doit être surveillé et recommandé à la Police.

J'ai l'honneur d'être avec le plus profond respect de Votre Excellence

Monseigneur   Le très humble et
                       très obéissant Serviteur
                       Le Général chef de l'Etat-major Gén.al
                       Bon de la Martinière

S. E. Mr. le Ministre de la Guerre Duc de Feltre

79

At all events, he got the information, so vital to Wellington, that Napoleon was coming up the road from Paris to Philippeville and intended to cross the river Sambre at Charleroi, through the gap in the Belgian defence system between the fortress at Mons and the broken country of the Ardennes.

Grant immediately sent this information to Wellington at Brussels. His messenger was intercepted by a Hanoverian cavalry patrol and taken to Major-General Dörnberg, commanding the cavalry screen on the frontier. Dörnberg read Grant's message, on which so much depended, and returned it to him with the comment that 'so far from convincing him that the emperor was advancing for battle, it assured him of the contrary'.

By the time Grant received this and had ridden himself, like a madman, to get the information to Wellington, the desperate encounter battle at Quatre Bras had already begun. So, because of the opinion of a German officer, one of the great decisive battles of history had to be fought in the muddy rye fields on the slopes of Mont St Jean at Waterloo, instead of on ground far more suitable for Wellington's purpose on the banks of the Sambre at Charleroi.

The incident is a classic illustration of the utter uselessness of the best information if it arrives too late. It is also a reminder of the perennial problem encountered by most intelligence officers at some time or other in their careers: they can obtain vital information, but they cannot always persuade people to believe it.

CHAPTER EIGHT

The Great Peace and Civil War

After the fall of Napoleon, Britain's position was even stronger than it had been at the end of the Seven Years' War, and the achievements of her navy and army in the battle for survival against the French emperor had completely eclipsed that unfortunate reverse when the American Colonies gained their independence. Wellington and the reputation of his invincible troops dominated the peace conference – the Congress of Vienna – and the prestige gained in the Peninsula and at Waterloo encouraged the British to feel they had come to the end of the second Hundred Years' War with France. There was now no power in Europe capable of affecting the development of the empire whose foundations had been laid in 1763.

As if to mark this confidence – though in fact underlining the congenital reluctance of British politicians to spend money on the armed forces – ships were laid up, regiments were disbanded, and military intelligence completely disappeared. One or two clerks remained in what had been the Depot of Military Knowledge, to dust the shelves in the library and hold the key of the map store, but no attempt was made to pursue the original concept – that intelligence should be collected and studied in peacetime so that the country would be prepared for war.

Colquhoun Grant and Andrew Leith Hay were relegated to half pay; John Waters, more fortunate, remained on the administrative staff. The other member of the famous quartet, Charles Somers Cocks, had been killed at the siege of Burgos in 1812.

There was a similar decline in political intelligence. Surrounded by the sea and protected by the Royal Navy, Britain turned her back on continental affairs and showed little or no interest in what went on across the Channel. Spies were not needed in peacetime.

This attitude was not common to the rest of Europe, where all the alterations made to the map, first by Napoleon and then by the Congress of Vienna, aroused undercurrents of nationalism, envy and animosity. Continental nations, sharing land frontiers and often harbouring minority groups of other nationalities, had a constant need to know the capabilities and intentions of their neighbours, though some, like Austria and France, do not seem to have attached much importance to the information.

Therefore, although in England there was not a great deal of employment for the secret agent, on the continent the traffic in secrets in the courts, ministries and departments continued to provide business for those attracted by a hazardous occupation, and useful supplements to the salaries of unscrupulous government servants. Paradoxically, the existence of this clandestine commerce was no secret, but it seems to have been unobtrusive, and there were no great scandals, no revelations and no memorable names attached to it until the appearance of the Prussian spymaster, Wilhelm Stieber, in the 1860s.

The four decades after Waterloo were called by the Victorians the period of the 'Great Peace', simply because Britain was not involved in warfare in Europe. During this period she was building her empire. Her army and her navy were undermanned, underpaid, neglected and indeed ignored by the majority of politicians and the nation as a whole; yet land forces, taken to theatres of operations by the Royal Navy, fought in Burma, Afghanistan, China, New Zealand, Africa and India. Intelligence played very little part in these campaigns. Since there was no General Staff, 'information' was the responsibility of the Quartermaster-General's department – as it had been, ever since James II combined the duties of the Scoutmaster and the Harbinger – and the whole subject was regarded as being well within the scope of mounted patrols or scouts. Although some use was made of local inhabitants, natives were seldom trusted and there were usually language problems.

In these circumstances it is not surprising that the story of the British empire is punctuated with such surprises as the slaughter of the Kabul Garrison in 1842, the Indian Mutiny, and many disasters and

'The remnants of an army.' Surgeon William Brydon, sole survivor of the retreat from Kabul (1842), is seen reaching Jellalabad in Lady Butler's famous picture. A classic illustration of the result of an absence of intelligence.

massacres in areas as widely separated as the Fish River in British Kaffraria and the mouth of the Peiho River in China.

Thus, when the Eastern Question – a euphemism for the designs of many European nations on the corpse of the Ottoman empire – brought England, France, Turkey and Sardinia into an alliance against Russia in 1854, to prevent the Russian occupation of Constantinople (Istanbul), it is understandable that nothing was known of the future area of operations.

Part of the fault lay in the widely held opinion that intelligence of this sort is a function of war, and only of war, despite the stated policy of Frederick Duke of York when he founded the Depot of Military Knowledge. The real trouble was that, yet again, the British government had been taken by surprise, and there was no intelligence link between the Foreign Office, the Admiralty and the War Office.

A military intelligence organization, of a sort, was hastily contrived and run, initially by a civilian named Charles Calvert until he died of overwork and cholera, and all through the war anyone connected with intelligence had to contend with a prejudice openly admitted by Raglan, and expressed in the words of the official history of the Crimean War, that 'the gathering of knowledge by clandestine means was repulsive to the feelings of English Gentlemen'.

Nevertheless, the need for intelligence was obvious and imperative. This was recognized by the War Office and, after Lord Raglan's death in June 1855, Lord Panmure constantly urged his successor, General Simpson, to spend more on it. 'Intelligence', he wrote, 'is of such infinite value in every way that it ought to be had.'

The administrative chaos of the war revealed to the British public, with a total disregard for security, by war correspondents such as William Howard Russell of *The Times*, also exposed the neglect of intelligence. One of the results of the war was that the principles of the Depot of Military Knowledge, set up more than fifty years before, were re-examined and re-applied to a department in the War Office. This, to a varying degree as the years passed, was thereafter dedicated to military intelligence.

William Howard Russell, whose investigative journalism during the Crimean War led the Tsar to say, 'We have no need of spies, we have *The Times*.'

America did not plunge into the cataclysm of the War of Secession without any experience of political or military intelligence, and for those who wished to study the subject there was much to learn from Amherst and Washington. Benjamin Tallmadge's spy ring had been very effective, but it had not been manned by soldiers, nor was it primarily concerned with military information.

The first American intelligence service designed purely for military purposes was that of Generals Zachary Taylor and Winfield Scott, who mobilized what were officially known as Spy Companies in the Mexican War of 1846–7. These companies were formed to 'commit irregular operations against the Mexicans', and the use of the word 'operations' raises some doubts about their role in espionage; possibly they were guerrillas rather more than spies. However, they certainly did a great deal of spying, and it may be noted that, in recruiting them, Generals Taylor and Scott unwittingly observed the principle laid down by Genghis Khan – spies must either be indigenous to the country in which they are to operate, or of a nationality different from the force they support – thereby reducing the risks of suspicion and identification.

The Spy Companies were manned by Mexicans and Indians of the border tribes, restless by nature and willing to undertake the tasks allotted to them because of their liking for money and adventure – the motive of most spies. As it turned out, their services were valuable; General Scott's success in assaulting and taking Mexico City was largely the result of accurate and timely information supplied by his Spy Company.

The Spy Company system was an example of intelligence raised and run purely in support of local military operations. It was disbanded when the war ended, and there appeared to be no further need for it. Thus when the Civil War – the War of Secession – began in 1861 there were no intelligence, counter-intelligence or even federal police systems in the United States.

Civil wars can be and usually are happy hunting-grounds for the spy, because he can mix so easily with friend and foe, but America shared the English prejudice against spying. The Americans of the mid-nineteenth century were not prone to conspiracy; there still seemed to be room enough in their vast continent for many schools of thought and opinion – until the issues of slavery and secession defined the limits of toleration.

Intelligence systems cannot be set up overnight. It may be easy enough to appoint certain people to act as an intelligence staff; agents can be recruited and told what information they are to collect, but the actual acquisition of facts, and the interpreting of them, can be a long, difficult and delicate operation. Much depends upon being able to penetrate an espionage target by making contacts, gaining their confidence, and finally persuading them, by one means or another, to provide what is wanted. All this takes time. Thus, when war suddenly breaks out, as it did in America with the bombardment of Fort Sumter on 12 April 1861, and there is no organized intelligence system on either side, espionage has to be in the hands of amateurs and results are likely to be haphazard and irregular.

Yet although there was no proper military system, the nucleus of one did exist in the form of a private detective agency in Chicago, run by a Scotsman, Allan Pinkerton, far more famous as the progenitor of 'private eyes' in America than Thomas Phelips ever was for the same profession in England.

Called in by the president of the Philadelphia, Wilmington and Baltimore Railroad, it was Pinkerton and his invaluable assistants, Timothy Webster and Harry Davies, who thwarted the Secessionists' design for a certain 'Captain' Fernandina to assassinate Abraham Lincoln, the newly elected President, as he passed through Baltimore on his railway journey to his inauguration in March 1861. Lincoln was protected, but

again the problem of credibility recurred. Pinkerton had the greatest difficulty in persuading him that the danger was real.

After the Fernandina incident, Pinkerton was regarded as the obvious choice for the head of a Federal secret service when the war began, but he was not a success. He suffered from the same fault as the farm labourer who led the Duke of Monmouth's force into such difficulties at Sedgemoor: he could not appreciate the military significance of information he received, and in retaining his 'civilian' outlook he was convinced that spies must always be civilians. He may well have been a good detective; he was undoubtedly very competent in the field of counter-espionage, but he knew nothing of active, acquisitive intelligence or of the most elementary skills of movement and communication. If he had done, his best agent, Timothy Webster, operating in the 'rebel' capital of Richmond, would not have been hanged by the Confederates. This was the direct result of Pinkerton's inept efforts to find out why the previously steady flow of information had suddenly ceased. Webster had become seriously ill. Two Federal agents, Price Lewis and John Scully, were sent to find out what had happened to him, and they immediately attracted suspicion. Arrested, charged with

Allan Pinkerton, founder of the American 'private eye' system and Federal head of intelligence, stands with Lincoln and McClellan at Antietam, 1862. Despite the Napoleonic posture, Pinkerton's knowledge of military matters proved inadequate.

85

Field intelligence officers, American style. The Scouts and Guides to the Federal Army, October 1862.

espionage and threatened with the gallows, they betrayed Webster to save their own necks.

The Confederates held strong views about the proper way to dispose of enemy spies, in contrast to Federal, or Union, clemency which was probably inspired by Lincoln himself. Yet neither side executed women, and this may perhaps be one of the reasons why female spies and agents occupy so prominent a place in the story of espionage in the American Civil War.

In his book *The Craft of Intelligence*, Allen Dulles claims that intelligence did not really play any significant part in the Civil War, and that acquisition was more or less confined to local and temporary targets. In the light of such intelligence achievements as the breaking of the Japanese 'Purple Code' in the Second World War, this generalization is true enough, but it does no justice to the memory of men and women like Timothy Webster, Rose Greenhow, J. O. Kerbey, Belle Boyd, Lafayette Baker and, perhaps the most dedicated secret agent of them all, Elizabeth van Lew. There is plenty of evidence that timely information from Rose Greenhow materially affected the first battle of Bull Run, but one cannot judge the value of intelligence purely in terms of battlefield results. By this criterion the great commander Jef-

frey Amherst, for example, was not a superb military spymaster because, unlike Marlborough or Wellington, he had no Blenheim or Waterloo. Sun Tzu put intelligence in its right perspective when he wrote: 'To win one hundred victories in one hundred battles is not the acme of skill. The acme of skill is to reduce the enemy without fighting.'

It is not possible to calculate with any exactness the extent to which information supplied by spies influenced the decisions of rival commanders in the War of Secession, but we do know that it had a direct effect on operations; otherwise, for instance, that renowned Confederate General Stonewall Jackson would not have written:

24 May 1862

Miss Belle Boyd,
    I thank you, for myself and for the army, for the immense service that you have rendered your country today.

Hastily, I am your friend,
T. J. Jackson C.S.A.

She had discovered that Federal troops were planning to destroy certain bridges, thereby cutting the route of a Confederate relief column on its way to join Jackson. Belle ran across open fields under heavy

The first battle of Bull Run, 1861. Knowledge of the Federal route, passed on by the Confederate agent, Rose Greenhow, resulted in the rout of McDowell's troops.

Rose Greenhow with her
daughter in a
domestic pose.

fire from Federal infantry and artillery to carry her vital information
to the 1st Maryland Regiment and the Louisiana Brigade. The bridges
were saved.

The courage of such spies was extraordinary but, as was only to be
expected, they were unskilled amateurs whose passionate partisanship
added to the conventional risks of their undertakings – the women seldom made any effort to conceal their loyalties. Rose Greenhow, for
instance, was an attractive widow in her early forties, and a Washington socialite with a wide circle of influential friends. She had been
a great admirer of President Buchanan but heartily disapproved of his
successor, Abraham Lincoln. Living in the heart of the Federal capital,
she was in an ideal position to spy for the Confederates. Her 'handler'
was Lieutenant-Colonel Thomas Jordan, head of intelligence in the
Confederate army, and her success seems to have been due partly to
her willingness to take her more important informants upstairs and earn
their confidence and confidences, and partly to the treasonable lack
of security of the men who shared her bed.

One of her greatest coups was right at the beginning of the war, in
July 1861, when she obtained, and passed to the Confederate General
Beauregard, a copy of the Federal General McDowell's orders to the

Army of the Potomac for the advance into Virginia. On this information, Beauregard was able to concentrate his force on the routes to be taken by McDowell's troops, with the result that on 21 July the Confederate army not only defeated but put to flight the Federal force, which ran back to Washington in total confusion.

Although suspected of being a spy, dogged by Pinkerton and his men, and virtually imprisoned in her house on Sixteenth Street, Rose continued to entertain her intimate friends – such as James Buchanan the ex-President, Colonel Keyes the military secretary to General Winfield Scott, and Senator Wilson of Massachusetts, chairman of the US Senate Military Affairs Committee – and send the information they gave her to Colonel Jordan by her loyal couriers, among whom were Betty Duvall and Lillie MacKall. In the spring of 1862 Rose was locked up in Old Capitol Prison, but the flow of information continued, and late in May she was despatched, with a number of other suspects, to the Confederate capital of Richmond, Virginia. The Southern President, Jefferson Davies, sent her on a secret mission to England where she was received by Queen Victoria, invited everywhere, and wrote a bestseller on her adventures. Returning to America in September 1864 on the blockade-runner *Condor*, she was drowned when the ship, chased by a Federal gunboat, ran aground off Wilmington, and the small boat in which she tried to get ashore capsized in heavy seas.

Lafayette Baker was a Federal spy who posed as an itinerant photographer – even though his camera was broken – and he wandered round Confederate units, particularly officers' messes, collecting information for General Winfield Scott and pretending to take pictures. It was a role which today would invite arrest practically on sight, but in those

Federal mortars near Yorktown, 1862. On both sides the pleasure of appearing in a photograph took precedence over the need for security.

days he was looked upon as merely an unusual type of pedlar. Eventually his failure ever to deliver the photographs, for which so many bewhiskered young men in the grey uniforms had posed so carefully, led his disappointed customers to suspect his interest in them and their conversations. He was arrested in Fredericksburg and confined in a jail from which he escaped at once, filing through the bars of a window. Reporting back to General Scott, he was commissioned, rose to be a Provost Marshal in charge of intelligence and counter-intelligence, and was eventually promoted to the rank of Brigadier.

Belle Boyd, a Confederate spy, was only seventeen when the war began. She lived in Martinsburg, Virginia, and publicly established her attitude to the Union when invading Federal troops attempted to raise their flag on her parents' house. Belle's mother objected and tried to slam the front door in the face of a Union soldier. When he kicked the door in Belle lost her temper and shot him with a pistol. The unfortunate man died and Belle, protected by the provisions of martial law, successfully pleaded justifiable homicide. Despite this incident, which must have indicated a certain degree of unfriendliness – if nothing more – towards the Union cause, a New York journalist and several Federal officers were billeted in the Boyd house. Unwittingly, they provided Belle, an ardent eavesdropper, with a mass of useful military information, which she passed on. There is no evidence that she ever adopted Rose Greenhow's methods for obtaining it.

With the strange chivalry, or perhaps gallantry, peculiar to this war, Union newspapers portrayed this enemy agent as a paragon of skill, beauty and courage when she made the irretrievable mistake of entrusting an intelligence report intended for General Jackson to a courier who was in fact a Union agent. She was imprisoned and later exchanged, being sent to Richmond, probably because she was a 'difficult' prisoner. She too went to England and, like Rose Greenhow, was treated as a heroine, but on her return she was taken prisoner again, this time by Samuel Wylde Hardinge, a Federal naval officer commanding a blockading gunboat.

They fell in love, returned to England and were married on 25 August 1864 at St James's, Piccadilly. Hardinge, for some reason not entirely clear, went back to America and was at once arrested and charged with conniving at the escape of the Confederate captain of the ship in which Belle had returned from England. Hardinge died in prison. Belle, widowed at the age of twenty-one, later went on the stage and died in Wisconsin in 1901.

One of the first analysts in the history of signal intelligence – the monitoring, by one means or another, of enemy signal traffic – was J. O. Kerbey, who in peacetime had been a railroad telegraph operator. When the war began he supported the Union cause and, having told his friends in Washington that he was 'going South to see what he could see', he happened to be behind the Confederate lines just before the first battle of Bull Run. Watching the withdrawal of Confederate troops from positions that, with the aid of tree trunks and brushwood, had

Hardinge, B. B.

BELLE BOYD,

IN

CAMP AND PRISON.

With an Introduction
BY A FRIEND OF THE SOUTH.

IN TWO VOLUMES.

VOL. I.

LONDON:
SAUNDERS, OTLEY, AND CO.,
66 BROOK STREET, W.
1865.

Memoirs of a Confederate spy. Belle Boyd's autobiography was a best-seller in Victorian England.

Belle Boyd, a heroine of the War of Secession.

been made to look from a distance like batteries of artillery, he realized he had information of the greatest value to the Federal Army of the Potomac. He tried to get to its headquarters, only to be stopped on the way and taken into custody as an enemy agent. No one believed what he tried desperately to tell them – and there was no reason why they should. A freelance spy with no credentials volunteering information of that sort is not likely to be believed – the trap seems too obvious.

Shortly afterwards, still wandering about with no definite aim, he was again taken prisoner, but by a Confederate officer. Kerbey then offered his services as a railroader, and on the orders of General Beauregard he was sent down the line to the rear. Subsequently he tapped telegraph lines in Richmond and sent his information out by letter, using the secret communications system devised by Elizabeth van Lew for getting messages to Washington. His code was simple enough. He wrote what seemed to be a perfectly innocent letter to a friend in the North, but on the paper were a few apparently accidental pen scratches and small blots which were in fact a number, such as three, five or nine – in Morse code. This indicated that the hidden message in the letter was composed of every third, fifth or ninth word in the text. Kerbey was later commissioned into the Federal army as a second lieutenant, and he survived the war.

Strangely enough the most valuable spy working for the North against the South was a Southerner, Elizabeth van Lew. She lived in Richmond, surrounded by Confederate friends, and yet was prepared to betray them, spy on her neighbours, jeopardize the lives of the soldiers of her State, risk her own life and that of her mother and brother under frequent threats of 'lynch-law' violence, and ruin her family financially, all for one reason: she had a fanatical hatred of slavery.

Born in 1818, she was forty-three at the outbreak of war, and her feelings as an 'abolitionist' had been known ever since her return from school in Philadelphia, when she had freed the van Lew slaves. Throughout the war she was suspected of being against secession and disloyal to the Confederacy – she was known to be against slavery – but the people of Richmond could not believe that a Virginian aristocrat could really be capable of actively opposing the cause for which so many were prepared to die, and did. They assumed she was mad. They called her 'Crazy Bet'. What seems so extraordinary is that although everything she did was regarded as suspicious, no one in Richmond seems to have penetrated behind her craziness to find that she was the supremely efficient controller of the best and consistently most reliable and effective espionage system established for either side.

She worked for General George H. Sharpe, Chief of the Federal Bureau of Military Information, and between the van Lew house and General Sharpe's headquarters she set up five secret relay stations on a secret communication system which never broke down. Most of the intelligence from the Richmond area received by General Ulysses S. Grant and his predecessors in command of the Army of the Potomac came either from or through her, and it was Grant who said to her, 'You have sent me the most valuable information received from Richmond during the war.'

In Elizabeth van Lew's house there was a secret room under the roof, approached through a door hidden behind a chest of drawers. Its existence was suspected but never discovered, despite many attempts to find it by Confederate counter-intelligence search parties. In it she concealed Union spies, agents and escaped prisoners of war, such as Colonel Paul Revere, until they could be got out along her secret ways.

Like Walsingham, she financed her organization almost entirely out of her own pocket, and at the end of the war her claim for repayment of 15,000 dollars spent on Union intelligence was countersigned by General Grant. She did not receive one cent either of pay or of her claim, and though under Grant's presidential administration she was made postmistress of Richmond, this was later reduced to a minor cleri-

The *Intrepid*, an observation balloon used in 1862. Early balloons rotated continuously, inducing sickness in the observers and making concentration impossible.

cal post in the same department. Because of her wartime activities Richmond society would have nothing whatsoever to do with her, and she spent the last years of her life in miserable poverty, existing on the generosity of relatives of Colonel Paul Revere, grateful to her for concealing him in her secret room. The ageing Negro servants she had freed so many years ago remained with her to the end. They did not share the deep-rooted prejudice against spies.

The wounds of this fearful war healed slowly. It had been an unpleasant shock to many Americans to discover how divided they were and how easy it had been to recruit spies. Politicians and military leaders had learned a lot about intelligence, its value, and ways of acquiring and passing it. Observer balloons had been used for surveillance, though not for the first time (the English had employed them for the same purpose in the Napoleonic Wars). The electric telegraph had passed messages at great speed over long distances, although the Union spy Kerbey had shown how vulnerable it was without the protection of codes and ciphers.

For the first time, railways had played a major part in the movement of troops and war material and, also for the first time, elaborate trench systems had been constructed for purposes other than the siege of a town – foreshadowing the trench warfare of 1914–18. The pattern of war was changing. The days of the slow-firing unrifled musket and cannon were over, and new weapons involved new tactics. The pattern of intelligence was changing too, but the man who at this time did most to affect its development – and increase the prejudice against it – was not an American but a German.

93

CHAPTER NINE
Bismarck's 'King of Sleuthhounds'

As a spy, and as a spymaster, the talents of Wilhelm Johann Karl Eduard Stieber, born in the small Prussian town of Merseburg on 3 May 1818, three years after the battle of Waterloo, have never been surpassed, but whereas others of his calling were sometimes compelled by force of circumstance to descend to contemptible, cruel or vicious measures to attain their ends, Stieber began at that level and remained there, untrammelled by conscience, ethics or inhibitions.

Although his parents wanted him to be a priest, Karl Stieber became a lawyer and rapidly acquired a large and profitable practice in Berlin. When only in his late twenties and early thirties, between 1845 and 1850, he defended no less than three thousand clients and secured a very high rate of acquittals. He thus achieved a reputation as a liberal-minded protector of criminals and the oppressed working class. Yet, during all this time he was not only a police spy but the anonymous editor of the local police gazette. From these functions he gained inside information on the tactics his legal opponents would adopt in court, a factor which largely accounted for his forensic success.

As a police informer he first appeared on the record in 1845, when he denounced as a dangerous revolutionary a man named Schloeffel, who trusted him and confided in him, and who was his wife's uncle. The episode illustrates Stieber's *modus operandi*.

To be a successful police spy, able to provide accurate information on disturbers of the peace, Stieber had to establish himself not merely as a helpful lawyer of radical views, but also as an active supporter of the radical elements which appeared from time to time in the streets of Potsdam – greatly to the alarm of King Frederick William of Prussia who, ever fearful of assassination, had not inherited the strength and decision of his Hohenzollern forbears. Stieber had to be accepted and trusted by the mob, yet at the same time he wished to bring himself to the notice of the King as an ardent monarchist. His chance came during the riots of 1848.

Joining a particularly dangerous-looking mob surrounding the terrified King, Stieber got close enough to him to whisper that all was well. There was nothing to fear because His Majesty was under the protection of Stieber the spy and a large number of his agents. He thus gained the King's notice, gratitude and confidence and, in 1850, the post of

Opposite, Wilhelm Stieber, the rarely acknowledged intelligence genius behind Bismark's imperialist foreign policy.

commissioner of police. From then on, Stieber's loyalty to the Prussian monarchy and the principles of absolutism remained steadfast. His aims were clear-cut: to root out and destroy all traces of republicanism, and to advance himself to a position of unassailable authority.

Five years later, in 1855, Frederick William was certified insane, and the regent who replaced him, later Kaiser Wilhelm I, made it clear that in his opinion Stieber's appointment in the police force was indisputable proof of his predecessor's state of mind. As soon as the royal favour was withdrawn, Stieber's enemies, of whom he had acquired a large number in thirteen years of minding other people's business, made a concerted effort to have him dismissed from the police and excluded from the Bar. But when he was brought to trial on a long list of charges, he completely out-manœuvred the prosecution and established that he had done nothing without royal authority. The royal authority was now under close medical supervision, and the court could do nothing against Stieber without also condemning the unfortunate King. Stieber was acquitted. He was also dismissed and advised to take a prolonged holiday, preferably in another country.

His holiday lasted from 1858 until 1863, and he spent most of it in Russia. While commissioner of police in Berlin he had been able to cover up an awkward scandal involving a Russian diplomat, and this was either remembered, or brought to notice again by Stieber himself, when he went to St Petersburg. There he was given the task of reorganizing the Tsar's secret police, the Ochrana, which he extended to include a system of keeping in close touch with all suspected political or criminal offenders seeking sanctuary outside Russia. In effect he developed an external department of the Ochrana, which remained in existence until 1917.

During the years of his exile Stieber never ceased spying for his own country, collecting a great deal of detailed information on Russia and all the countries he visited while employed by the Tsar. This is sometimes quoted as evidence of his innate patriotism, but it is more likely to have been forethought in providing himself with a marketable commodity which could be exchanged for a return ticket to Prussia. As things turned out, he had no difficulty in going back, for in 1863 he was presented to Prince Otto von Bismarck by a newspaper proprietor who recommended him as a 'useful man'. This meeting was the beginning of a strange partnership which was to last until Stieber's death, twenty-nine years later. Bismarck depended on Stieber for the information on which he based his plans and decisions for creating the German empire. Stieber depended on Bismarck for his authority, his social aspirations, and protection from his enemies.

Bismarck had decided that the reduction of Austria would be the first act of his imperial drama, and when he asked Stieber to undertake an 'investigation' into the military capabilities and state of readiness of Austria, the latter accepted with enthusiasm. Hitherto most of his energies and skill as a spy had been applied to the suppression and persecution of radicals and republicans. He had no experience of military intelligence, nor had he any military training. It would therefore be reasonable to assume that, like Pinkerton, Stieber might prove to be of little value when it came to evaluating military information. But he was a German, tirelessly methodical, thorough and painstaking. He dealt primarily with facts, and when he drew conclusions from them he supported those conclusions with more facts. He seldom speculated. He made certain.

To these Teutonic traits he added a cynical realism in appraising his fellow men. He travelled everywhere in Austria as a pedlar, riding in a cart containing his wares in two large boxes. In one were statuettes of the Holy Family and the Saints; in the other were pornographic pictures. He calculated that the 'prospect' who brushed aside the statuettes might well be interested in the alternative.

He remained in Austria for months, without ever arousing suspicion, and when he returned he brought back for the Prussian staff a mass of material so complete and accurate that General Helmuth von Moltke was able to plan with confidence a campaign lasting only seven weeks, and ending with the total defeat of Austria at the battle of Sadowa on 3 July 1866.

Sadowa (1866) marked the culmination of Stieber's work in Austria. On the left the Prussians' 'needle-gun' has a devastating effect, while the Austrians continue to use the old muzzle-loading musket.

It must not, however, be imagined that all the credit for this remarkable achievement should go to Stieber. Intelligence, by itself, cannot win a battle. One of the most important factors in the Prussian defeat of the Austrians was the possession, by the Prussians, of a new breech-loading rifle (called the needle-gun) which had a rapid rate of fire, was accurate up to a range of 500 yards, and could be loaded while the firer was lying down. The Austrians had only the muzzle-loading musket, unchanged in essentials for 150 years. They lost 40,000 men; the Prussians had 9,000 casualties. The figures speak for themselves.

In his report, Stieber had given all details of Austrian weapons and tactics, and no doubt they influenced von Moltke in the timing of his attack – before the Austrians could re-equip with a better infantry weapon. But, as has been said, it is not the function of intelligence to take decisions; Stieber provided the information which helped von Moltke to make up his mind.

The value of all the pre-campaign intelligence prompted Bismarck to raise a special unit of secret police, commanded by Stieber (who was still a civilian), to operate in the field on active service. It had two main functions: the protection of important personages such as the King, Bismarck himself, army commanders and senior staff officers; and the 'neutralizing' of enemy intelligence services. It was the first German counter-intelligence unit, modelled on Fouché's system of counter-spies, and it had Stieber's own innovations. He was entirely ruthless in insisting on the immediate execution of anyone suspected of spying on the Prussian army, and he introduced strict censorship of all despatches, telegrams and correspondence sent by the army in the field. Although it was later to become a vital part of intelligence machinery, censorship was not strictly necessary in the victorious Prussian army, but it added greatly to Stieber's personal power. The scrutiny of private and other correspondence by officials – the means by which so many spies have been caught – was going on long before Alexander the Great, but Stieber appears to have been the first to organize it on a regular, formal and overt basis.

He also instituted what he called a Central Information Bureau, which published regular and widely distributed bulletins dealing mainly with enemy losses and misfortunes. This was an aspect of 'disinformation' designed to raise and maintain the morale of troops on active service, and has since become an important element of psychological warfare.

Although today psychological operations (psyops) and propaganda form no part of the intelligence function, those who conduct this type of warfare rely heavily upon intelligence to give advice on what form of propaganda or psyops theme is likely to be most effective.

The success of the Austrian campaign restored Stieber to royal favour. Bismarck called him 'my king of sleuthhounds'; nearly everyone else feared, hated and shunned him. To the King and Bismarck, the only superiors he acknowledged, Stieber was obsequious and servile; to all other Prussians he was brash, bombastic and assertive. But though his progress to power had been rapid, he still remained stationary at the foot of the social ladder, burning with a sense of injustice.

The French republicans who had overthrown the 'Citizen-King' Louis Philippe had themselves been overcome in 1852, when the royal house was restored in the person of Napoleon III. It was now becoming increasingly clear that Bismarck's dream of a united Germany could not be achieved without a confrontation with France – if only because the prospect of German unity had been a nightmare to French rulers and statesmen for centuries. Between 1866 and 1868 Bismarck and Stieber worked together on the problem of war with France. Napoleon, on the other hand, studied the lessons of the American Civil War and the Austrian disaster at Sadowa. At his instigation the French *chassepot* rifle and *mitrailleuse* machine-gun were produced, giving France an advantage in weapons over Prussia.

In 1868 Stieber and his two principal subordinates, Kaltenbach and Zernicki, set out to ensure that the Prussian victory over France would be as swift and certain as the conquest of Austria. They lived in France for eighteen months, unmolested, and not only completed an intelligence survey on a scale never previously attempted, but recruited and briefed a large number of local agents for use when the invasion began. Such people, lying dormant until they were needed, would today be called 'sleepers'.

In Berlin the French military attaché, Colonel Baron Stoffel, learned of Stieber's mission in France and found out a great deal about German preparations for war. But the frequent and detailed reports and warnings he sent to Paris merely earned him a reputation as an alarmist.

Stieber had gone to France under a weight of personal responsibility far greater than most spies have to bear. His chief task was to assess the new French weapons against the whole background of the French attitude to war, and their support for the current regime. In effect, he was to advise Bismarck and von Moltke whether or not invasion was feasible, and therefore his estimates of French 'war potential' had to be accurate.

When rumours of Prussian intentions began at last to filter into the French Chamber of Deputies, and there was some anxiety, the Minister for War insisted that the French army was ready, 'down to the last gaiter button'. Stieber and his agents knew that this assurance was based on wishful thinking.

From Stieber's point of view all the omens were good, and a less methodical spy might well have accepted them. His chief contribution to intelligence as a discipline is the fact that he was the first high-level spy who, though on a military assignment, attached equal importance to non-military matters, and refused to be satisfied with hearsay evidence or impressions. He delved deeply into the patriotism and politics of the people living in the area of future military operations. He studied commerce and agriculture in relation to such things as productivity, local grievances and the level of taxation. At the same time he collected topographical details, especially in terms of communications and

After Sedan (1870).
Slumped in a defeat that
was largely the result of
Stieber's work, Napoleon
III accepts humiliation at
the hands of Bismarck.

obstacles such as rivers, canals and defiles through hilly country. He located fortifications, assembly areas, factories producing war material, dumps and depots. He covered every conceivable subject bearing on the operations and administration of an invading force.

Having collected all this material, he then collated and analysed it, and in coming to conclusions which inevitably had to take certain imponderables into account, he based them on the worst case – making proper allowances for mistakes and miscalculations. All this careful processing of material, which filled three large trunks of Stieber's baggage when he returned to Berlin, would have been a credit to any modern intelligence staff.

France and Germany, equally to blame, declared war on 17 July 1870. Just over six weeks later, on 1 September, Napoleon III and his staff surrendered to the Prussians at Sedan. The campaign was a triumph for Prussian Intelligence, staff duties and artillery.

It was Stieber who was responsible for the deliberate policy of *Schreck-lichkeit* (literally, 'frightfulness') which reappeared in 1914. He held the view that it was the duty of a spy to kill an enemy spy in the same way that soldiers killed one another on the battlefield. Hence his counter-intelligence took the form of a murderous secret warfare aimed at the physical destruction of the enemy's intelligence system, and in France a great many innocent men and women were shot or hanged simply because curiosity brought them to a window to watch a troop train or a battery of artillery go by. Such ruthlessness inevitably invited retaliation, but Stieber had no interest in the fate of his own agents, and never attempted to protect them. He took the view that it was their responsibility to look after themselves.

There are many stories of Stieber; of his unscrupulous use of women agents who were required to be 'good-looking and not fastidious', and of his notorious 'Green House'. This was a place of private entertainment in Berlin which catered for every kind of vice, depravity and perversion, but was primarily reserved for people of consequence who, on indulging their fancies, were grabbed and held by the claws of blackmail. It is possible that Stieber, the perpetual *parvenu* who suffered genuinely from social isolation, also used the Green House to try and blackmail the nobility and aristocracy into accepting him, but he never succeeded. Bismarck and the Kaiser decorated him no less than twenty-seven times for his services to Prussia and the German empire, but he remained the man whom no one of importance wanted to know.

He died in 1892, and representatives of many of the rulers and much of the aristocracy of Europe went to his funeral. This must have been gratifying to his widow, but it was said at the time that they came in excellent humour, not to pay their respects but to assure themselves that he was really dead.

The Germans were not proud of Stieber. His methods, ruthlessness and inhumanity were deplored during his lifetime, and for years after his death his name was never mentioned, particularly in military circles, for two reasons: he had left a stain upon the honour of the Fatherland and, more important still, his intelligence activities would, if they became widely known, detract from the glory of Prussian arms. Nevertheless, his achievements were considerable. He had proved again what Mithridates had discovered centuries before, that good intelligence makes it possible to gain the maximum success in the shortest time and with the least risk. In addition, he developed censorship and psychological warfare, setting out the pattern for the Propaganda Ministry run by Dr Josef Goebbels in Nazi Germany, seventy years later.

Stieber was cold and calculating, a skilful amateur psychologist who understood how to exploit human weaknesses. He used fear, either directly or in the form of blackmail, to produce the information he needed, and at the same time give protection to himself and his masters. In France he evolved a 'Fifth Column' in the invasion area long before the term was invented (in the Spanish Civil War of 1936–9) and he also foreshadowed the tactics of the *Blitzkrieg*, the lightning war – not by using tanks and dive bombers but by providing the operations staff with information so accurate and detailed that the way to victory lay open before them. He did not invent ruthlessness and terror, he organized them, and ever since then they have been generally regarded as inevitable elements of a secret service. Practically every seed he planted in the fields of intelligence and counter-intelligence has since grown into a sturdy tree. Above all, he created a new climate of fear, suspicion and intrigue in Europe. Long afterwards, in his *History of the World War*, Liddell Hart wrote, 'Fifty years were spent in the process of making Europe explosive; five days were enough to detonate it.' It was Stieber who placed the first caches of gunpowder.

In the period between Stieber's death and the beginning of the First World War the intelligence services of all European countries intensified their activities. Germany was now the threat because she had upset the balance of power. No one seriously believed that the Prussian armies, having proved their strength and skill, would hereafter be content with ceremonial parades and field exercises with blank ammunition. Even England became alarmed by what had happened at Sedan and the Siege of Paris and, under the great Whig reformer Lord Cardwell, began to tidy up the War Office and sweep the dust out of the Intelligence Department.

One overt means whereby nations endeavoured to keep an eye on one another was the system of service attachés, instituted in Paris in 1850. By attaching experienced regular officers to the diplomatic team manning the embassies in foreign capitals, it was hoped that home governments would be able to tap a variety of sources and receive useful information in the diplomatic bag. The scheme worked, but there were problems. Life in embassies was expensive. In many cases this limited the choice of attachés to officers with considerable private means, who were not necessarily suitable for the post. Furthermore, under all the diplomatic euphemisms it was perfectly obvious that an attaché was simply an accredited spy, a fact underlined by the behaviour of a great many of them; and in the middle of the nineteenth century it was not easy to get rid of an undesirable without creating an international incident.

Russian attachés were always suspect, right from the beginning; a case in point was that of Colonel Zantiewitz in Vienna. Though guilty of espionage and bribery he could not be arrested, and in the end the Emperor Franz Josef had to be deliberately discourteous to him to indicate that his presence was no longer acceptable. The Colonel took the hint and arranged to be recalled. In 1911 another of his countrymen, Colonel Bazarov, made himself unwanted in Berlin and was escorted to the frontier. He was following in the footsteps of his immediate predecessor, Colonel Michelsen, to whom the same thing had happened. A certain Major Delmastro of the Italian embassy in Vienna in 1906 was not able to finish his tour of duty. Major (Lord) Kitchener of the British

Lord Kitchener, an early exponent of the 'great game', made secret maps of Palestine which contributed to Allenby's victory in 1917, nearly thirty years later.

army took advantage of an attachment in Turkey to make secret maps of Palestine, later of great use to Allenby in his Palestinian campaign in 1917. Kitchener was not detected; nor was Colonel Baron Stoffel who had done so much good work for France when he was in Berlin – but, as we have seen, like many other intelligence officers, Stoffel could not make his government believe him.

Probably the most fully documented case involving a military attaché and espionage is that of the German attaché Colonel Max von Schwartzkoppen and Captain Alfred Dreyfus of the French General Staff in Paris in 1894. It is a long, involved and discreditable story of the persecution of an innocent and outstandingly able Jewish officer, Dreyfus, by a disgraceful combination of government ministers, senior army officers, clergymen, newspapermen and the French middle class, who, on the basis of a comparison of handwriting which ought not to

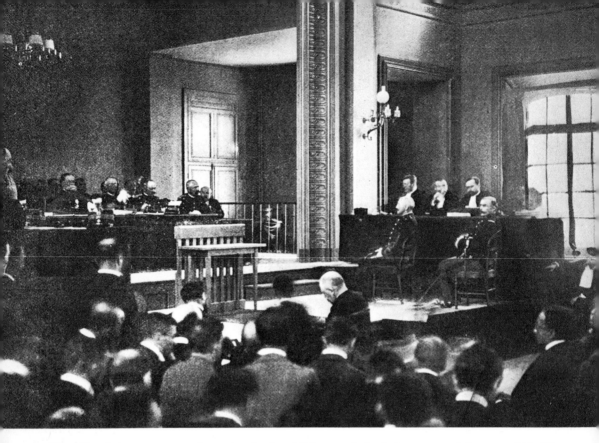

Alfred Dreyfus,
photographed at his court
martial during the
reading of the accusation.

have deceived a child, sent their victim to spend the rest of his life on
Devil's Island – the penal settlement off the northern coast of South
America. Thereafter, the persecutors of Dreyfus turned their attention
to the handful of honest men, among whom were Émile Zola and
Georges Picquart, who were convinced Dreyfus was innocent and
laboured to see justice done. Fortunately, all was well in the end.
Dreyfus and his faithful supporters were reinstated, and the guilty
either fled or committed suicide; but the effects lingered on, reviving
all the fears implanted by Stieber and his agents.

In England at this time the Intelligence Department largely relied,
in collecting military information on foreign countries and their armies,
on a type of young officer neither unique nor unusual, who for the first
time – and with considerable irresponsibility – was given active
encouragement and payment for expenses to pursue interests with
which the army refused to be associated. Wearing plain clothes and
outwardly addicted to such hobbies as archaeology, botany or the collection of butterflies, these young men wandered all over Europe playing what Kipling called the 'great game', and gazing apparently with
the innocent interest of tourists at fortifications, beaches, parades and
manœuvres, and anything else that 'might be of value'. Since they were
untrained amateurs, and few were ever properly briefed to obtain the
answers to specific questions, they frequently got into trouble. Captains
Trench, Brandon and Stewart were arrested and imprisoned in Ger-

many – though as a gesture of goodwill they were released at the time of the wedding of Kaiser Wilhelm II's daughter. Captain Count Gleichen of the Grenadier Guards thoroughly recommended the sport of what he called 'fortress hunting', saying that 'the added risk of fines and imprisonment gives a delicious zest to it'.

Young Robert Baden-Powell early in his career justified the motto subsequently adopted by the movement he founded. Trying to get close enough to see a new machine-gun being tested on a range in Berlin, he was seen by a sentry. He at once produced a bottle of brandy, feigned drunkenness, invited the suspicious soldier to join him in a drink and went away leaving the impression that he was a harmless tourist who had lost his way. Later he adapted his talent for painting water-colours to military purposes; his pictures of coastal scenes in Algeria contained the new defences round the port of Bizerta, concealed in a code of dots and dashes. In Dalmatia he drew careful pictures of local butterflies in which veins on the wings represented lines of fortified outworks, and dots of various sizes denoted the calibre of the guns.

It was all very exciting for those who took part. Some of the information they brought back was useful, but nothing was really organized or co-ordinated, and too much depended on good luck. Nevertheless, it showed that in England, as on the continent, the collection of material on potential enemies and areas of operations was becoming increasingly important.

One of the more remarkable spies of this period did not look upon himself as a spy at all yet, since dedicated journalism has much in common with espionage, it can be said that Henri Georges Stephan Adolphe Opper de Blowitz, covering the Congress of Berlin in 1878 for *The Times* of London, was indeed a spy for his newspaper. He succeeded in obtaining all the details, every day, of an extremely secret conference under the noses of Bismarck and Stieber, and publishing the final Treaty of Berlin on the morning of the day when it was to be signed. This achievement is startling enough, but he owes his place in this brief record to his scheme for obtaining information from his accomplice, who was one of the delegates. He never met him anywhere, never posted anything, never exchanged documents, and never even appeared to know anyone who could be an accomplice or an intermediary. Yet the method was so simple that it never occurred to Stieber's 'shadows' who kept him under constant surveillance. De Blowitz and his accomplice wore hats of exactly similar pattern and approximately the same size. Each day they dined at the same restaurant at about the same time, sitting as far apart as possible, and on leaving they merely exchanged hats on the hatstand. De Blowitz took away the one in which a report of the day's proceedings was tucked in the inner band.

In his time, Stieber had been an active member of the fraternity of *agents provocateurs*, and he had also brought the Ochrana, the Tsarist secret police, to a high standard of potency. It all seems to be part of the pattern that the most notorious *agent provocateur* and police spy in

Opper de Blowitz, the *Times* correspondent who outwitted Stieber himself, shown with the hat that acted as a 'letter-box' for top secret information.

A spy relaxes. Ievno
Azeff, the *agent provocateur*
who engineered the
assassination of his own
minister of the interior,
enjoying himself with a
friend.

Russian history should have been a member of the reconstructed
Ochrana. His name was Ievno Azeff.

Azeff first got into trouble in 1892, at the age of twenty-three, in
his home town of Rostov on the Don. He evaded the police, escaped
to Karlsruhe in Germany, and enrolled at the Polytechnic for a course
in electrical engineering. When he ran out of the money he had stolen
in Rostov he wrote to the Ochrana, offering his services as a spy in
the external department founded by Stieber. Accepted, at a salary of
fifty roubles a month, he began work among the revolutionary societies
of Russian expatriates living in Germany. They believed him to be an
ardent terrorist, yet he was so valuable to the Ochrana that he was
eventually called to Moscow to work directly under its chief, Zubatov.
Here he at once began to infiltrate the underground revolutionary
organizations, and became known to them as the ideal man of action –
someone prepared to practise terror as well as to preach it.

Apparently with the connivance of Zubatov he plotted and actually
carried out the assassination, first of the Grand Duke Sergius, uncle
of the Tsar, and then of Plehve, the much-hated minister of the interior
nominally responsible, among other things, for the Ochrana. Zubatov
seems to have regarded these two victims as expendable in the cause

of justifying to the Tsar the need for the Ochrana, and of allaying any suspicion of Azeff among the revolutionaries. Plehve took no precautions against assassination because he was confident that Zubatov – and Azeff – would protect him. Azeff himself delighted in the slaying of Plehve because he had instigated an appalling pogrom at Kishenev; and Azeff was a Jew.

However, in condoning active terrorism by one of his agents, Zubatov had gone too far. A particularly industrious revolutionary named Burtzev discovered the truth, and the deception recoiled upon Zubatov and the Ochrana with devastating effect. Azeff fled back to Germany. He happened to meet Burtzev in Frankfurt in 1912 and complained bitterly that Burtzev's inquisitiveness had prevented him from achieving his lifelong ambition – the assassination of the Tsar.

The worst traitor of the nineteenth century was an Austrian, Colonel Alfred Redl. He features in many books on espionage as the man who handed over to Russia the Austrian Operational Plan III, thereby causing the death of tens of thousands of his countrymen in the opening campaigns of the First World War. Redl was a spymaster in that for a long time he was in charge of Austrian intelligence, and therefore responsible for the spies and agents employed by his department. Even in this capacity he was a traitor because he deliberately concealed from the operations staff certain Russian intentions which put the Austrian plans at risk. He was not, however, a spy since, like Benedict Arnold, he was entitled to possess the information he passed to the enemy. He was an enemy agent, and his case is of particular interest because it is one of the early examples of a form of blackmail in which Stieber specialized and which the Russians use.

Redl was an active homosexual at a time when homosexuality was a crime; and since it was a crime, gratification of his needs was risky and therefore expensive. He needed a great deal of money. The Russians discovered his private interests and were prepared to provide it, on conditions. Once in the net, there was no escape. He was finally caught by his own system of postal censorship, part of his efficient counter-intelligence organization. Two of his subordinates became suspicious of a package addressed to 'Opera Ball 13', and containing nothing but a large sum of money in notes, which had been delivered to the poste restante section of the General Post Office in Vienna. On 31 May 1913 it was claimed by Redl. Following an afternoon of intense but concealed activity, four senior officers called on Redl at midnight. When they went away, leaving a Browning pistol lying on the table, Redl wrote two letters, one to his brother and the other to the army commander who had trusted him. He also left a note:

Levity and passion have destroyed me; pray for me.
I pay with my life for my sins.
1.15 a.m. I will die now. Please do not permit a post mortem examination. Pray for me.

Alfred Redl, the Austrian spymaster whose homosexuality made him a target for Russian blackmail.

In 1914, when the Austrians went to war against the small Serbian army led by Marshal Putnik, who had heard all about Plan III from the Russians, the Austrian army was cut to pieces in a series of battles and suffered 500,000 casualties. Redl had known this would happen.

Depending on the context, intelligence can be either the product resulting from the processing of information, or it can be an organization, and even the activities of that organization. By the end of the nineteenth century there had been great changes in all three aspects, and they had come about largely because of the French Revolution. Before 1789, wars had been fought mainly by small professional forces for limited political or territorial ends. The armies of the French Republic turned war into an international conflict requiring all the resources of the nations involved.

Previously, intelligence had been divided into two main categories, political and military. Marlborough, for instance, had kept the distinction, and each category was handled by a separate staff. Napoleon had left political matters to Fouché while Schulmeister dealt with military intelligence, but the categories were already merging. Stieber, the civilian, completed the fusion. He collected everything that bore on his masters' intentions and poured it all into the same pot, simply because in his mind it was all directed towards a single purpose – the total defeat not merely of the enemy army but of the enemy nation.

Since war had become a national responsibility, intelligence had to follow suit. During the nineteenth century it was taken out of the casual hands of spies, agents and double agents, working for spymasters whose only means of control was financial, and given to professionals. Even so, the acquisition of information by clandestine means was still regarded by the British as unsporting, and by the Americans as something worse; it was un-American.

CHAPTER TEN

Prelude to war

The British had carried out a large number of military reforms after the shock of the Franco-Prussian War but, as usual, they had provided so little money for the Intelligence Department that it remained no more than a handful of officers and clerks occupying a few rooms in the War Office building in Whitehall. Even so, it provided the government with extremely accurate reports on the Boer preparations for war – all of which were ignored.

When the war began in October 1899 there was no field intelligence organization except for an advanced party of ten volunteer, and largely untrained, intelligence officers – among whom was Baden-Powell, later to be the hero of Mafeking. After the Boers' initial attack, these men found themselves besieged in Kimberley, Mafeking and Ladysmith, and General Redvers Buller, sent from England to restore the situation, found no intelligence staff in South Africa, though there was one intelligence officer, a second lieutenant, waiting for him at the docks in Cape Town.

Buller set out to relieve the beleaguered garrisons, and the three separate columns of his force suffered heavy defeats at Stormberg, Magersfontein and Colenso between 10 and 15 December 1899 – the Black Week – mainly because there was no effective intelligence system and also because the Boers could shoot fast and straight. A local native and a colonial scout offered Lord Methuen some useful information just before the battle at Stormberg, but he refused to make any use of it because it conflicted with his personal opinion.

Above, 'In the soup'. A contemporary German postcard of the Boer War shows the result of a refusal by the British government to believe accurate information supplied by the Intelligence Department. *Left*, Baden-Powell seen here on the trail in South Africa – an autobiographical self-portrait.

The founder of MI5.
Major-General Sir
Vernon Kell, KBE, CB,
who started the
department as a junior
captain in 1909, and ran
it until 1940.

As the war went on, an excellent 'Field Intelligence Department', the FID, was developed by Colonels George and David Henderson. New techniques and new organizations were evolved; good use was made of balloons for observation and of pigeons for swift communications. Signal intelligence again became important, and a new aspect of this was to send signalmen under the line of sight of Boer heliographs to read the winking messages in Morse.

The whole highly professional organization was disbanded immediately the war ended, but Colonel David Henderson wrote the first military intelligence manual, *Field Intelligence, Its Principles and Practice* (1904), setting out his recommendations for 'an Intelligence Department organized so that in the case of war it can be expanded rapidly'. He was thanked and congratulated. Nothing was done. At length, in 1913, a certain Captain Macdonogh – one of the great names in British military intelligence – began to compile a register of men suitable for an intelligence corps when war broke out.

Rather more effort was devoted to counter-intelligence. One descendant of the police force originally raised under the provisions of Sir Robert Peel's Act of 1829 had been the Special Irish Branch, formed to deal with Irish terrorists who were planting bombs in many places in London during the middle of the nineteenth century. Having achieved its objects – for the time being – the Special Irish Branch was retained as a separate department of the force to deal with security of the realm in direct relation to espionage, subversive organizations and sabotage. The word 'Irish' was dropped.

In 1909 the War Office suddenly realized there was no staff branch responsible for dealing with foreign spies operating in England, and a sub-committee of the Committee of Imperial Defence authorized a 'Special Intelligence Bureau' as part of Military Operations 5 (MO 5). A junior officer of the South Staffordshire Regiment named Captain Vernon Kell was allotted a tiny office, made to sign for two tables, two chairs and a cupboard, given the services of one clerk, and told

Brigadier-General David Henderson, author of the first intelligence pamphlet, escorting the politician William Joynson-Hicks on a visit to headquarters in 1913.

to start work. He was given no detailed instructions because no one was quite sure what he was supposed to do. Very sensibly, he went to see Superintendent Patrick Quinn of Special Branch, who was a very great help to him, and their first joint operation was an unqualified success. It took place in 1910, when Kaiser Wilhelm II came to London, to the funeral of King Edward VII.

Various unobtrusive people responsible for the Kaiser's safety were interested to note that among his retinue was a captain of the Imperial German Navy, known to be the acting head of German naval intelligence. They were even more interested when this distinguished officer took a cab to a barber's rather seedy little shop in the Caledonian Road, which for the past sixteen years had been run by Karl Gustav Ernst, technically a British subject because he had been born in England. Kell obtained permission for the barber's mail to be examined, and it transpired that he was what is known as a 'letter-box'. German intelligence sent him packages which contained letters, bearing British postage stamps, addressed to their resident spies in England. All Ernst had to do was open the packages, post the letters and in due course forward any replies to Germany by the same means – a service for which he was paid £1 a month.

Kell and Quinn, like Walsingham and Thurloe before them, made no move until the net was full. For the next four years the German espionage system in England was kept under careful surveillance by Special Branch and Kell's 'Bureau' – which became Military Intelligence 5 (MI5) – and within a few hours of the declaration of war, on 4 August 1914, Ernst and nearly all the German spies who had been operating in England were quietly taken into custody.

Until 1878, when the Treaty of Berlin caused another crisis of nationalism in the Balkans and Germany began to turn herself into a great naval power, their Lordships at the British Admiralty had not felt it necessary to concern themselves either with a naval staff or with naval intelligence. Having changed their minds, they spent the next thirty years trying out different organizations. Finally, when Winston Churchill became First Lord of the Admiralty in 1912, the staff structure he imposed contained departments of War Information, War Plans and War Arrangements under a Chief of War Staff. The Director of Naval Intelligence was the senior member of the naval staff and had direct access to the First Sea Lord. The Royal Navy had realized that if Britain was to maintain her position in the world, intelligence was of some importance.

Thus, at the beginning of the First World War, Naval Intelligence was properly organized, Special Branch, run by Sir Basil Thomson, had a great deal of experience, and MI5 had been in existence for five years. Admittedly, the total strength of MI5 at this time was only four officers, three 'investigators' and seven clerks, but, through its close links with Special Branch, it could call upon all the uniformed police forces of Great Britain. On the other hand, the acquisition of intelligence by 'ground forces' – Stieber's *forte* – lagged far behind.

Sir Basil Thomson, head of Special Branch at the outbreak of the First World War.

It was not until 1912 that the Special Intelligence Section was formed to take over responsibility for the activities of British agents overseas. Raised by Commander Mansfield Cumming (usually referred to as 'C') this Section subsequently became MI6. The funds originally allocated to it were meagre and it had very little time to make its presence felt before the war began. Naval Intelligence had its own somewhat static organization of informants and, for operational intelligence, relied chiefly on the interception of enemy signals traffic – provided the codes and ciphers could be broken. Soon after the war began, it was taken over by Admiral Sir Reginald 'Blinker' Hall – so called because he had a slight tic in one eyelid. The army had an intelligence department in the War Office and had drawn up mobilization plans, but it had no Intelligence Corps. This was to be raised as soon as mobilization was ordered, though there might be very little time to train it. Yet, because of the foresight of men like Colonel David Henderson, General Sir Henry Wilson, Director of Operations in the War Office, and Major – later Major-General Sir George – Macdonogh, the plans worked.

The state of German intelligence has been revealed by Colonel Walther Nicolai, who commanded the German intelligence service throughout the war. In his book *The German Secret Service* he says that since the war was regarded as a purely military affair, likely to be over in a few weeks, all intelligence responsibility rested with the Military Intelligence Department. He goes on to make a statement which illustrates the extraordinary prejudice against intelligence, which was not confined to England and America:

> Of the few officers trained in the secret service the best were rewarded by being released for work on the regimental staffs, and the remainder were shared among the army commands as Intelligence Service Officers. ... Strong scepticism prevailed in the army commands regarding the possibility and the usefulness of espionage in mobile operations. This went so far that one army command, on the advance through Belgium, left the Intelligence Officer behind in Liège as needless ballast.

It seems clear that Stieber and all his works had been carefully buried, and this time no civilian spy would be able to steal any of the glory of conquest from the army. Many officers followed the example of Erich von Ludendorff, and did not conceal their dislike and contempt for civilians. Nicolai points out that although, in the course of their studies and exercises based on the famous Schlieffen Plan for the invasion of Belgium and France, some attempt was made to estimate possible demands on the intelligence service, the elaborate war games dealt only with strategy and tactics. Such subjects as economic or political conditions in enemy states, or propaganda – which Stieber had investigated so carefully – were never discussed, and 'a world-wide intelligence service had never been the subject even of theoretical consideration'.

Military deficiencies were not made good by Germany's civilian spies. A fortnight before war was declared there were twenty-seven of them in England, most of whom were sleepers who had been living in the country for many years. One of them, Dr Karl Graves, was already in prison. He had been arrested in Glasgow in 1912 and tried and sentenced in Edinburgh. No doubt he felt he had been unlucky, because it was only in the previous year that Kell, with much difficulty, had persuaded the legislators to amend the Official Secrets Act of 1889 and make espionage in peacetime a punishable offence.

Another was Gustav Steinhauer, who subsequently wrote a book with the title *Steinhauer: The Kaiser's Master Spy*, a description which expressed his personal opinion. He travelled round, visiting various agents such as Kronauer in Walthamstow, Schappman in Exeter, Otto Weigels in Hull and Georg Kiener in Edinburgh, and then sent all of them a postcard on which was a veiled warning to be ready for war.

A rare photograph of Colonel Walter Nicolai, head of German intelligence throughout the First World War.

Since he had reason to believe some of them were being watched, this was not quite what one would expect of a 'master spy' – it would have been better if he had called himself a spymaster, which is not the same thing at all.

As a result of his warnings, Kronauer, Weigels and Schappman all returned to Germany feeling they had been compromised and it was not safe to remain. Steinhauer himself also got away, but Ernst the barber and twenty-three others hitherto at liberty were all requested to accompany polite police officers in the early hours of 5 August. Because of this round-up, no news whatsoever of Britain's mobilization, or of the move across the Channel of the British Expeditionary Force, reached Germany. It was a great surprise to General von Kluck and his First German Army, trying to feel their way round the left flank of the French Fifth Army, when the forward elements encountered the rapid and accurate fire of British troops near Mons.

'Am I surrounded by dolts?' said the Kaiser furiously, when he heard of this. 'Why have I never been told that we have no spies in England?'

It might be imagined that after the frightful experience of their defeat in 1870, and all the uproar over Dreyfus twenty-four years later, the French would have been abnormally 'intelligence-conscious'. They were, but practically all their efforts were devoted to counter-intelligence. Even when they had a thoroughly reliable former non-commissioned officer named Lajoux working as a double agent, providing the Germans with spurious information while he spied for France, they did not trust him, despite an impeccable record, and hounded him into exile in South America. Intent on keeping enemy spies out of France, little effort seems to have been made to find out what was happening beyond the frontier, with the result that, as Liddell Hart says in *The Real War*, 'the fundamental flaw in the French plan was that the Germans had deployed twice as many troops as the French Intelligence estimated, and for a vaster enveloping movement'.

The Belgians spent virtually no money at all on intelligence until 1912, largely because their neutrality had been guaranteed by treaties. After that date, some knowledge of the Schlieffen Plan and rumours of the manufacture of huge 16-inch Skoda siege artillery revived their interest in espionage, and it is said that one of the agents they then employed obtained all details of the new German guns. Thus the subsequent appearance of weapons of this calibre was not, to some people, the surprise it is said to have been. Nothing was done with this information because it was felt to be too late and it would have been too costly to strengthen the fortifications of Antwerp, Liège and Namur.

Just before the war, the Russians were spending 12,000,000 roubles (£1,250,000) a year on intelligence. Some of this went to people like Colonel Alfred Redl who were agents, and traitors, in target countries, and a great deal was spent on internal secret police, spies and informers. These date from the hated Oprichniks of Ivan the Terrible in the sixteenth century, through to the Ochrana, the Cheka, the OGPU, the NKVD, and finally the KGB and GRU of today.

The Russians seem to collect information mainly for the sake of collecting; like some quartermasters hoard surplus stores. They also seem to have been lax in keeping it up to date, and even after acquiring the enemy's plans, such as for example the Austrian Plan III, made little or no allowance for obvious alterations that would be made as soon as it was known they had been compromised. After Redl had shot himself the Austrian General Staff changed their plan as much as they could. These changes were anticipated by the Serbian Marshal Putnik but not by the Russians. In battle, Putnik was extremely successful; the Russians were not.

Despite their concentration on intelligence and counter-intelligence they showed disastrous negligence in one obvious aspect of military security, perhaps because the whole concept was so new. Their defeat at the hands of the Germans on the Eastern front was very largely the result of their failure to encode their operational wireless traffic. The German commanders were told, in clear, all they wanted to know.

The telegraph line which could be tapped, as it had been in South Africa and in the American Civil War, had hitherto provided a great deal of useful information, but with the invention of radio, signal intelligence rapidly assumed a position of paramount importance.

The Japanese did not enter the competitive field of international intelligence until their war with Russia in 1904–5, nor did they share the Asian tradition of exercising political control through an army of spies and informers. The ruling caste preferred to govern directly, without aids which they considered were beneath their dignity. The Japanese people were brought up to accept the divinity of their ruler, honour their ancestors, and obey without question the orders of their superiors. Until recently, there was no requirement for a domestic secret service, and when they at last recognized the need for intelligence and espionage in the fields of diplomacy and war, the spirit of self-sacrifice, so abundant in their agents, compensated for inexperience. They learned fast and were more thorough in their methods than even the Germans. For example, a Japanese clerk arrested by the Ochrana in St Petersburg in September 1904 had improved his 'cover' by becoming a diligent member of the Russian Orthodox Church and marrying a Russian woman.

The majority of important missions were undertaken by officers of the army and navy, who were quick to appreciate that the Western tendency to regard all Orientals as classless, identical 'natives' could be exploited. They did not hesitate to submerge themselve in the lower, faceless levels of Oriental humanity and take on the most menial tasks. The lowly clerk caught in St Petersburg was a senior naval officer. Even in 1939 one of the 'native' staff of an officers' mess in Singapore, a man named, Shawan, was known in Japan as Colonel Tsugunori Kadomatsu.

Profiting from a superficial resemblance to Chinese and Mongolians, Japanese spies in the guise of barbers, cooks, labourers and servants

of Russian officers and NCOs penetrated every part of the Russian garrison long before any military attack was made on Port Arthur. The organization of their espionage system was excellent, from the staff level where collected information was processed and disseminated, down to communications which included cut-outs and dead-letter boxes.

A cut-out is a link inserted in a line of communication for protection of the system. Thus a spymaster, for instance, writes a message and puts it in a dead-letter box (a hiding-place of any convenient sort which can be anything from a hollow tree to a safe deposit or, as in the case of de Blowitz, a hatband). It is collected by a cut-out courier who takes it to another dead-letter box where, in due course, it is collected by the spy. There can be many variations on this theme, but the principle is that the cut-out knows nothing except that he has to pick up a sealed package from one place and leave it in another. He does not even know anyone in the organization, except possibly the man who recruited him.

Having delayed their entry into the world of espionage until the beginning of the twentieth century, the Japanese grasped two of the basic principles almost at once. One is the need to centralize control, and the other is that any intelligence system must be put out on the ground and made fully operational long before any shooting starts. So, guided by their experience in their defeat of the Russians, and having determined after centuries of isolation to become a great world power, the silent probing tentacles of Japanese Intelligence began to feel their way round the globe.

In 1885 the American Secretary for War asked the Adjutant General for certain information about a foreign country and was told there was no department of the army capable of producing it. The Military Information Division (MID) was formed forthwith. It consisted of one officer and one clerk – reminiscent of the British MI5 – and was attached to the

Japanese Intelligence prepared the way for the destruction of Russian shipping at Port Arthur, 1904–5. The event is depicted by the artist Toshidide in traditionalist style.

Miscellaneous Branch of the Adjutant General's office. Its functions were to collect and file information forwarded by embassies overseas and culled from foreign newspapers.

Four years later, when the military attaché system was approved by Congress (it had been operating in Europe for thirty-five years), regular reports began to come in from London, Paris, Berlin, Vienna and St Petersburg. The quality of these reports varied considerably because, as in Europe, the officers who wrote them had been selected on the basis of private income rather than military capabilities. No allowances were provided to cover all their extra expenses. By 1892 the MID had justified its existence and the War Department gave it a charter: it was to collect and classify information on foreign countries, brief officers going to posts overseas, and keep a check on the state of readiness of reserve forces in America.

When the Spanish-American War began in 1898, Colonel Wagner was head of MID, the number of military attachés had increased to sixteen, and from the one in Madrid had come a great deal of useful information bearing on the war. Wagner at once prepared a careful assessment of the terrain, climate and operational conditions in Cuba – the basic intelligence needed for operational planning – and he recommended postponement of any invasion until the winter months in order to reduce what would otherwise be heavy losses from disease. President McKinley endorsed his view. Alger, Secretary for War, was furious – with Colonel Wagner. Like many a politician he was not particularly concerned with soldiers' lives, and had his own reasons for wanting swift action.

'You have made it impossible for my plan of campaign to be carried out,' he told Wagner. 'I will see to it that you do not receive any promotion in the army in the future.'

This was the first open expression of official prejudice; it was not the last. Colonel Wagner was in fact promoted, years later, by Congress, who made him a brigadier-general when he was on his death-bed.

Probably the best-known intelligence event of the Spanish-American War was the feat of Lieutenant Andrew S. Rowan of the 9th Infantry who, on the strength of having written an impressive book on Cuba – without actually visiting the island – was chosen by Wagner to make contact with the leader of the Cuban guerrillas, General Garcia. After an extremely hazardous journey, Rowan reached the guerrilla hideout on 13 April 1898 and brought back information which enabled Garcia and the American force commander, General Shafter, to co-ordinate their efforts against the Spanish. Twenty-two years later, Rowan was awarded the Distinguished Service Cross for this exploit.

A rather more important event at this time is the appearance in American intelligence history of Captain Ralph H. Van Deman. He was assigned to MID early in 1898 and later posted to Cuba, where he developed an enthusiasm for intelligence that was to continue unabated until his death fifty-five years later, in 1953. Van Deman was the true founder of American military intelligence, for without him

Wagner's organization would have perished. In keeping it alive Van Deman was constantly in arms against the familiar prejudice. There were many American counterparts of those British politicians and military leaders who, for generations, had argued that intelligence is underhand, unpleasant, unnecessary, and merely creates jobs for military misfits.

Van Deman's first brush with authority occurred in the Philippines, when he upset General Franklin Bell who was then the Provost Marshal. An American citizen named Robinson appeared to have become entangled with Japanese Intelligence, and as an earnest of his loyalty he had handed over certain documents to the American authorities. General Bell told the Commander-in-Chief, General MacArthur, that the right and proper thing to do was to return them. Van Deman, who had earned MacArthur's confidence through discovering and foiling a plot to assassinate him, advised against this. The documents were retained and Bell, accustomed to getting his own way and vindictive by nature, treated the minor incident as a personal slight.

In 1907, Bell became Chief of Staff to the army, and it was suggested to him by the commandant of the Army War College in Washington that, for convenience and economy, the MID could be moved from its location on Jackson Square into the new War College building. Bell took this a stage further and gave instructions for the MID to be absorbed into the War College, so that what had become the Second Section of the General Staff lost its identity and independence, and virtually ceased to exist as an intelligence unit. This happened in 1908, just at the time when Europe was beginning to slide down towards war and the Japanese were starting purposeful investigations of the American Pacific coast. This was demonstrated by the 'accidental' grounding of the Japanese battleship *Asama* in Turtle Bay, California, while her officers 'explored' the area around.

Major Van Deman was not in Washington at the time when Bell tried to get rid of intelligence. He had attended a course at the War College in 1906 and had then been sent to China to reconnoitre and report on lines of communication. He soon discovered that Japanese agents, so plentiful in the Pacific, were all over China. He returned to Washington in 1915, appointed to what was now called the Information Branch of the War College. He found it had deteriorated into a few unoccupied offices where the intelligence reports and telegrams from military attachés and other sources all over the world – including the expedition which General Pershing was leading against the bandit Pancho Villa in Mexico – were piling up, dusty and unread, because there was no one to read them.

Virtually single-handed he brought order out of the chaos and introduced a system for collating the reports, summarizing them, and distributing information and intelligence to branches of the staff which had a need to know. The war in Europe had been going on for more than a year; there was always a possibility that America would be

Captain Ralph H. Van Deman, the real founder of American military intelligence.

drawn into it, and yet there was still no intelligence staff or service. Van Deman's campaign for reviving the MID failed to arouse any interest.

Even when the United States came into the war in 1917, Van Deman was unable to persuade the Chief of Staff, General Hugh Scott, that armies in the field had been known to benefit from the services of an intelligence organization. Scott's view was that if, against his deepest convictions, such a thing did become necessary, it would be provided by the British and the French. Van Deman continued to press the point until Scott lost his temper, refused to discuss the matter or even see him again, and gave him a direct order not to approach the Secretary for War.

Van Deman then enlisted the help of two friends, a woman novelist and the chief of Washington police. They told the Secretary what the position was, and thereafter events moved at a staggering speed. Within forty-eight hours Van Deman was in charge of a newly formed Military *Intelligence* Branch – for the first time, 'Intelligence' replaced 'Information' to come into line with the terminology of the Allies – and he had been provided with the authority and the funds to put his designs into effect.

By this time, America had been at war with Germany for more than a month.

CHAPTER ELEVEN

The War to end War

Although parsimonious politicians had, over the centuries, enabled the armed services of Great Britain to acquire a reputation for total unpreparedness at the beginning of every war, the situation in August 1914 was a startling exception. This was mainly because even the politicians could not delude themselves into thinking there would be no explosion. Mobilization was smooth and swift; as we have seen, counter-intelligence swept up the German spies overnight. Everything was planned and ready, including a small operation designed to exploit the comparatively new and vital source of information – enemy signal traffic.

A few hours after the declaration of war, the British cable ship *Telconia* put to sea, made for a point just off the Dutch coast, found and winched up to the surface the submarine cable carrying German telegraph communications with the outside world, and cut it. Several hundred yards of cable were then reeled in and the cable cut again, making the damage irreparable.

This forced Germany to use radio or send messages by cables controlled by her enemies, but, from the Admiralty's point of view, the success of the plan depended on being able to read German signals. No one could have foreseen the extraordinary piece of luck arising from an incident in the Baltic only three weeks later. On 26 August the German light cruiser *Magdeburg* ran aground in thick fog and was attacked, when the fog cleared, by the Russian warships *Bogatyr* and *Pallada*. Among the casualties picked up by the Russians was a dying German seaman clutching a weighted book which would otherwise have sunk like his ship. The book contained the German naval code which the Russian High Command, a little more co-operative then than it is now, offered to the Admiralty. Winston Churchill sent a destroyer to Murmansk to fetch it.

In October 1914 Admiral Sir Reginald Hall became the director of naval intelligence and at once began to develop his predilection for codes and ciphers in what became the legendary Room 40 in the Admiralty Old Building. His chain of radio monitoring stations along the southeastern coast of England read German signals without difficulty until early in 1915, when a new transmitter went on the air from

Admiral Sir Reginald 'Blinker' Hall, director of British naval intelligence in the First World War.

Brussels. One of Mansfield Cumming's MI6 agents was sent off to investigate. He returned with the information that the new code might be obtained from an Austrian clerk named Alexander Szek, born in Croydon and with relatives still living there. What followed seems to have been an affair in the Stieber tradition.

As a result of intense pressure applied to Szek and his relations, a copy of the code was made and handed over to the MI6 agent. Szek then disappeared completely, and his father later accused the British of killing him. Obviously it was essential to prevent the Germans from finding out that the code had been compromised – hence the laborious copying out of what could otherwise have been stolen – and there was only one way of making absolutely sure Szek did not tell them. It seems possible that Blinker Hall and Mansfield Cumming weighed the life of an Austrian clerk against the lives of thousands in the trenches of Flanders and France.

Wilhelm Wassmuss, the German romantic whose rallying of Persian tribesmen against the British during the First World War paralleled the activities of T. E. Lawrence in Arabia.

Another German code of the greatest importance was acquired by a stroke of luck comparable to the capture of the *Magdeburg*'s code-book. A young German consul named Wilhelm Wassmuss, stationed at Bushire in Persia, had decided not to return to Berlin at the beginning of the war, when the British began to move into the area. Instead, he rode off into the hills with the object of organizing the local tribesmen and fighting a guerrilla war which would affect British oil interests in the Persian Gulf. He was in fact the German equivalent of Britain's Lawrence of Arabia, who tried to make trouble for the Turks. Both have been called spies, and in a sense they were, but their primary role was sabotage.

The British put an ever-increasing price on the head of Wassmuss – it rose from £3,000 to £25,000 – but he was never betrayed by any Persian peasants or tribesmen because they refused to believe, so it is said, that any man was worth that much. Pursued relentlessly by British patrols, he was on one occasion forced to abandon his baggage when he fled. It was then learned that he was offering a considerable sum for the return of a tin trunk, which he thought had been taken by local inhabitants at the time of his escape. In fact the British had picked it up, found it contained only papers, and had sent it back to England. Blinker Hall now called for it and discovered a copy of the German diplomatic Code No. 13040.

Working in the centre of a web of listening radio operators and industrious cryptographers, Blinker Hall achieved his greatest success in the celebrated affair of the Zimmermann telegram – a classic example of how to exploit an intelligence 'plum' with proper regard for the background situation and current climate of opinion. In 1917 the opposing armies had reached a position of virtual stalemate on the Western front. The British Commander-in-Chief, Field-Marshal Haig, had informed the Cabinet that without substantial reinforcements he could no longer do anything more than hold his ground. President Woodrow Wilson had no intention of taking his country into the war, although throughout America there was considerable antagonism towards Germany, brought about mainly by the activities of German agents such as the naval captain Franz Rintelen von Kleist, who had established himself in New York in 1915, and for the next two years did his best to sabotage the shipments of war materials, particularly artillery ammunition, being sent to France. Kleist invented a delayed action incendiary device which caused fires in the coal bunkers of munition ships when they were far out at sea. To save his ship, a captain was forced to flood his holds, saturating the ammunition; this was the reason for the constant complaints from British gunners in France of 'dud' or prematurely exploding shells – notably in the great bombardment before the battle of the Somme in July 1916.

At the beginning of January 1917, the cryptographers in Room 40 presented Admiral Hall with a telegram sent by Artur Zimmermann, German Secretary of State, to the German ambassador in Mexico City. The gist of it was that Germany intended to begin unrestricted submarine warfare on 1 February and that, though it was hoped that the United States would remain neutral, if they did declare war there should be a German alliance with Mexico and a consequent invasion of the American States of New Mexico, Texas and Arizona. In addition, Mexico was to be persuaded to enlist Japan in this enterprise.

Hall realized at once that to lay this deciphered message on the desk of the American ambassador in London would be to invite the scepticism of Washington, if nothing more. He then discovered that a duplicate copy had been transmitted by the telegraph cable running from Copenhagen to England and thence to Washington, where Western Union had forwarded it to Mexico City. Having persuaded Western Union to cable a copy to the American embassy in London, he provided the embassy staff with the means of deciphering it. Thus he avoided any accusation of faking the telegram, and also concealed from the Germans the fact that the British had the German diplomatic code.

Opposite, The Zimmermann telegram. American reluctance to enter the First World War was overcome by British decipherment and exploitation of this message.

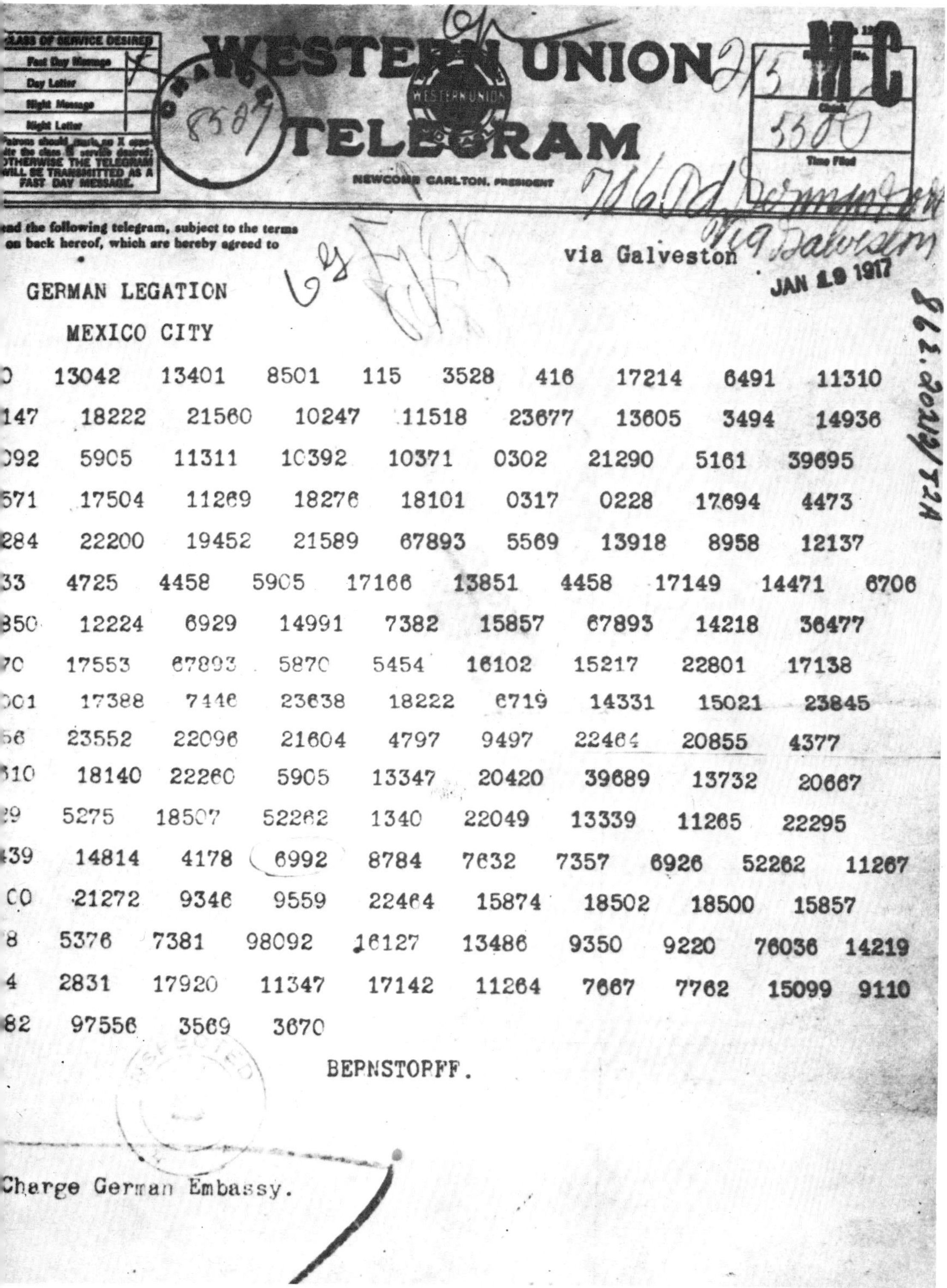

CLASS OF SERVICE DESIRED
Fast Day Message	✓
Day Letter	
Night Message	
Night Letter	

Patrons should mark an X oppo-
site the class of service desired;
OTHERWISE THE TELEGRAM
WILL BE TRANSMITTED AS A
FAST DAY MESSAGE.

WESTERN UNION TELEGRAM

NEWCOMB CARLTON, PRESIDENT

Send the following telegram, subject to the terms
on back hereof, which are hereby agreed to

via Galveston

JAN 19 1917

GERMAN LEGATION

MEXICO CITY

130	13042	13401	8501	115	3528	416	17214	6491	11310
147	18222	21560	10247	11518	23677	13605	3494	14936	
092	5905	11311	10392	10371	0302	21290	5161	39695	
571	17504	11269	18276	18101	0317	0228	17694	4473	
284	22200	19452	21589	67893	5569	13918	8958	12137	
33	4725	4458	5905	17166	13851	4458	17149	14471	6706
850	12224	6929	14991	7382	15857	67893	14218	36477	
70	17553	67893	5870	5454	16102	15217	22801	17138	
001	17388	7446	23638	18222	6719	14331	15021	23845	
56	23552	22096	21604	4797	9497	22464	20855	4377	
310	18140	22260	5905	13347	20420	39689	13732	20667	
29	5275	18507	52262	1340	22049	13339	11265	22295	
439	14814	4178	6992	8784	7632	7357	6926	52262	11267
00	21272	9346	9559	22464	15874	18502	18500	15857	
8	5376	7381	98092	16127	13486	9350	9220	76036	14219
4	2831	17920	11347	17142	11264	7667	7762	15099	9110
82	97556	3569	3670						

BERNSTORFF.

Charge German Embassy.

On 2 April 1917 President Wilson came to the Capitol and demanded war with Germany. Signal intelligence had changed the course of history.

Hitherto the number of women to achieve distinction in the history of intelligence was small, mainly because espionage was largely a man's world in which woman usually played the part of the seductress, employed by a combination of spymaster and pander, to extract information either in unguarded moments or as the price of pleasure. One of the better known agents in this category was Gertrud Margarete Zelle, also called Mata Hari, 'Eye of the Morning'.

Born in Leeuwarden, Holland, on 7 August 1876, she made a disastrous marriage with a Dutchman of Scottish extraction named MacLeod, and lived with him for a time in Java, where she became fascinated by the skill of Javanese dancers and the more erotic aspects of their art. When her marriage broke up she became a professional dancer, took the name of Mata Hari, and first appeared in Paris in 1905. She also became a courtesan remarkable for the quality of her performance because, unlike most professional prostitutes, she thoroughly enjoyed what she was doing.

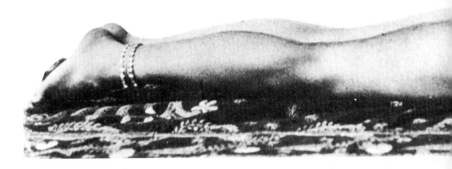

She then travelled about Europe, dancing and enjoying herself with a large number of men (who had to be of good class and position, for she was a resolute snob). When the war broke out in 1914 she happened to be in Berlin, where her principal friend was von Jago, the chief of police. He had made her acquaintance when calling to investigate a complaint that she performed certain of her dances clad only in a few bangles – which was true. They spent a lot of time together.

She was now thirty-eight, and her experience added to her attractions. She was also a congenital liar, cultivating an image of Oriental mysticism and living in a world of fantasy. It is not surprising that at the end, when she was telling the truth to try and save her life, no one believed her. She was on the books of Colonel Nicolai's organization as Agent H.21; she was also on those of Captain Ladoux in Paris; she had slept with Major von Kalle, the German military attaché and head of German Intelligence in Madrid ... it was all a tangle and a muddle. No one trusted her, she achieved no espionage *coups*, and it became obvious to everyone that she was loyal only to herself.

Arrested by the French on 13 January 1917 and charged with espionage, she became caught in her own lies, although Captain Bouchardon of the War Office, the prosecuting officer, soon realized that

Mata Hari ('Eye of the Morning'), real name Gertrud Zelle, the archetypal 'beautiful spy'. In fact she was an ineffective agent who died in front of a firing squad in 1917.

the case against her rested on little more than suspicion. But it is one of the many hazards of espionage that suspicion is usually enough. Early in the morning of 15 October 1917 she was taken to the moat at Vincennes, where she met the same fate as the young Duke d'Enghien. It is not easy now to penetrate the fog of legend surrounding her memory; for instance, it has been said that she was shot so that the headlines in the French press would divert public attention from reports of mutinies in the French army. At the time, the press of many nations expressed ironic surprise that the French, of all people, should have thus disposed of a woman so accomplished in intimate entertainment. The real point, however, is that amateur adventurers of either sex who play at being spies ask for trouble, and usually get it.

Another woman who had to face a firing squad was Edith Cavell—shot by the Germans in Brussels at dawn on 12 October 1915. She died with extreme courage (unfortified, as Mata Hari had been, by a glass of brandy), though she was not a spy but the organizer of an escape route for prisoners of war. Her execution had a great effect on opinion in America, for in that country they had made a particular point of not shooting women like Elizabeth van Lew, Rose Greenhow and Belle Boyd.

Another spy, Marthe Richer (*née* Bettenfeld), had a German-sounding name, but she was a French girl; nicknamed l'Alouette, the Lark, she was the first French woman aviator. After the death of her husband, a French officer killed in action early in 1916, she was recruited as a spy by one of his friends, who happened to be Captain Ladoux of the Deuxième Bureau. He sent her to Spain to penetrate the efficient German secret service operating there, and she became the mistress of Baron Hans von Krohn, the German naval attaché, who seems to have been genuinely in love with her. While in Madrid Marthe met Mata Hari, who was then calling herself Lady MacLeod and living with von Kalle, the military attaché in the German embassy. Ladoux had not told her that Mata Hari was supposed to be one of his agents. As a spy, Marthe was as capable and successful as poor Mata Hari was incompetent and unlucky. She sent Ladoux much valuable information on such things as German submarine refuelling points on the Spanish coast, and the secret routes used by German agents slipping through the Pyrenees into France. But she received no heroine's welcome when she returned to France at the end of the war, and was surprised to learn that most of the officers of the Deuxième Bureau had been shocked by her relationship with von Krohn. Like Schulmeister, she was to be rewarded only with gold. She went to live in England, married a man named Crompton, and lived happily ever after, though in 1933 her country at last acknowledged her patriotism by making her an Officer of the Legion of Honour.

Opposite, Marthe Richer, known as l'Alouette. In espionage terms she was far more successful than her better-known contemporary, Mata Hari.

Another woman whose activities have become almost as legendary as those of Mata Hari was a German, Elsbeth Schragmuller, also known as 'Tiger Eyes' and Fraulein Doktor—she had obtained a Doctorate of Philosophy at Freiburg University in 1913. Eager to serve her

Elsbeth 'Tiger Eyes' Schragmuller, the German Ph.D. who ran a school for spies in Antwerp.

country, she pestered Colonel Walther Nicolai for a post in his *Nachrichtendienst* (intelligence service) and was at length put in charge of a school for spies in the Rue de la Pepinière in Antwerp. It was an establishment almost as peculiar in its way as Stieber's Green House had been. Elsbeth seems to have been a sadist, and the students were said to be terrified of her. Locked in their rooms, known only by numbers, and forced to wear masks all the time, they were savagely disciplined for any infringement of her rules. With Teutonic zeal she carried security to ludicrous lengths, yet all her training was based on an elementary misconception.

She approached espionage from an entirely academic point of view – uninspired, unpractical and humourless – and thought she could thereby foresee all contingencies, and could therefore evolve a system of routine drills for dealing with any situation. She studied the mechanics of guile and listed the principles of furtiveness. She held firmly to the view that espionage was simply a matter of training; she would not believe it was also very much a matter of character, and innate, unteachable attributes such as common sense and resourcefulness.

The legends grew, turning this dull, dark, plain woman into a beautiful blonde German spymistress of superhuman ingenuity and skill, but her methods, and consequently her spies, were very unsuccessful. For example she sent two Dutchmen, Jenssen and Roos, to Portsmouth, where they were to become cigar importers, cabling their requirements to Rotterdam in a code that related Havanas and Coronas to British warships – 3,000 Coronas meant three battleships, and so on. Since neither the sailors nor the people of Portsmouth were noted for their high consumption of cigars, Vernon Kell's men from MI5 became interested when they learned, through postal censorship, that 48,000 had been ordered in ten days. Jenssen and Roos were arrested and shot.

With one exception – the extraordinary case of Jules Silber – German spies operating in England in World War One were not very successful. Another example was the unfortunate Carl Hans Lody, an officer in the German naval reserve who had a job in New York and had married an American girl. Lody made the mistake of visiting his parents in Hamburg just before the war began. Since men with his command of colloquial English were not easy to find, Nicolai persuaded him to become a spy. He landed in Scotland, and immediately compromised himself by announcing in a telegram to his contact in Sweden: 'Hope we beat these damned Germans soon.' An alert, and no doubt thrifty, Scottish postmaster, surprised that anyone should waste money on such a statement to someone in a neutral country, sent a copy to Kell. Thereafter it was merely a question of collecting evidence.

Lody, too, became part of the folklore of intelligence, even to the extent of being described, in one instance, as the 'spy who lost a war'. Apparently, he heard while in Dundee of Winston Churchill's unrealized plan to take the pressure off the British Expeditionary Force, retreating southwestwards from Mons, by bringing Russian troops from Archangel by sea to northern Scotland, taking them by train through England, and then landing them at Ostend. The rumour of Russian

Carl Hans Lody, the German spy whose report of Russian troops in England (the 'snow on their boots' story) may have cost the Germans a victory at the Marne, September 1914.

troops 'with snow on their boots' swept through England, gaining strength from 'eye-witnesses' who had probably seen troop trains travelling south with drawn blinds, filled with sleeping Scottish soldiers. Rumour became 'fact' in the light of such tales as that of the railway worker in the south of England, unfamiliar with the Scottish dialect, who asked a soldier on one of these trains where he came from, and interpreted the reply of 'Ross-shire' as 'Russia'. It is said that Lody passed all this as confirmed information to his Swedish contact, whence it ran through intelligence channels as far as General von Moltke, nephew of the Chief of Staff in the time of Bismarck. The result was that the Germans failed to win the decisive battle of the Marne in September 1914 because two divisions were withheld to counter the Russian threat from the Channel coast.

It is difficult now to discover whether there is really any substance in all this; if so, it is an interesting example of the power of rumour and of the inherent danger in relying upon one source without seeking confirmation from another.

The list of spies caught by postal and telegraph censorship is impressive, and underlines what has always been one of the spy's greatest problems: how to pass on his information without compromising himself.

Stieber's mantle lay where it had fallen at his death. He would have been horrified by the academic and 'modern' methods of Elsbeth Schragmuller and the blundering inefficiency of German espionage as a whole; but he would have been delighted with Jules Silber.

Silber was a German who had travelled all over the world, living for some time in South Africa where he had fought for the British in the Boer War. He had also lived in India and America, and was almost indistinguishable from an Englishman. In August 1914 he was in New York, and at once offered his services to the German embassy. His sole motive was patriotism, he sought no reward of any kind except victory for the Fatherland. He worked alone and developed his own techniques, suffering none of the disadvantages of the Schragmuller training, nor was he hampered by having to accept orders from Berlin. He had a natural genius for espionage, and he seems to have possessed all the qualities needed by the perfect spy.

He came to England without a passport (up to 1914 they were not required), but he had documents to prove his services to Britain in South Africa, and quite a number of influential contacts who were prepared to recommend him. His talents as a linguist, particularly in German, were of great help in getting him a job in the postal censorship department, which he knew was a source of great distress to German espionage. Being an unusually astute man he realized he could do nothing to rescue German spies entangled in the MI5 net, nor could he warn Nicolai of British spies in Germany without endangering himself. Any of the experts – Vernon Kell, Mansfield Cumming, Sir Basil Thomson or Admiral Hall – would have been quick to identify the source of such information, so he sat quietly at his desk, extracting information from the letters he was required to read, and one cannot help wondering, now, whether he saw any of the surprisingly indiscreet correspondence of Field-Marshal Sir John French to his mistress Mrs Winifred Bennett when, as the original commander of the British Expeditionary Force, he wrote to tell her of secret troop movements and the itineraries of people like King George V who went to France to visit him.

Silber despatched all his information from a room hired on the other side of London from his office and his lodgings. Here he photographed material, wrote his reports, and prepared the envelopes bearing the stamp 'Passed by the Censor'. He took the precaution of leaving the stubs of theatre and concert tickets in his lodgings, to explain his absences to his landlady.

His greatest achievement was the discovery of the British plan for 'Q ships', the carefully disguised armed merchantmen which were to blow so many German submarine raiders out of the water. The plan was revealed in the artless letter of a girl who wrote about her brother working on some peculiar scheme for putting guns and collapsible superstructures on old merchant vessels. Silber took a grave risk by

War Office.
Whitehall. S.W.1.

5th July, 1919.

Dear Silber,

At the termination of the Postal Censorship I wish to thank you for the work you have done in my Directorate.

The Censorship has inevitably worked to a large extent in the dark, and the public has even now little appreciation of the pressure which this weapon has enabled us to exert on the enemy, or of the part it played in winning the war.

You may, however, be sure that in the General Staff there is no lack of appreciation of the importance of the work to which you have given your services.

Yours sincerely,

Major General.
Director of Military Intelligence.

J.C. Silber Esq.,
5, Amberley Street,
Liverpool.

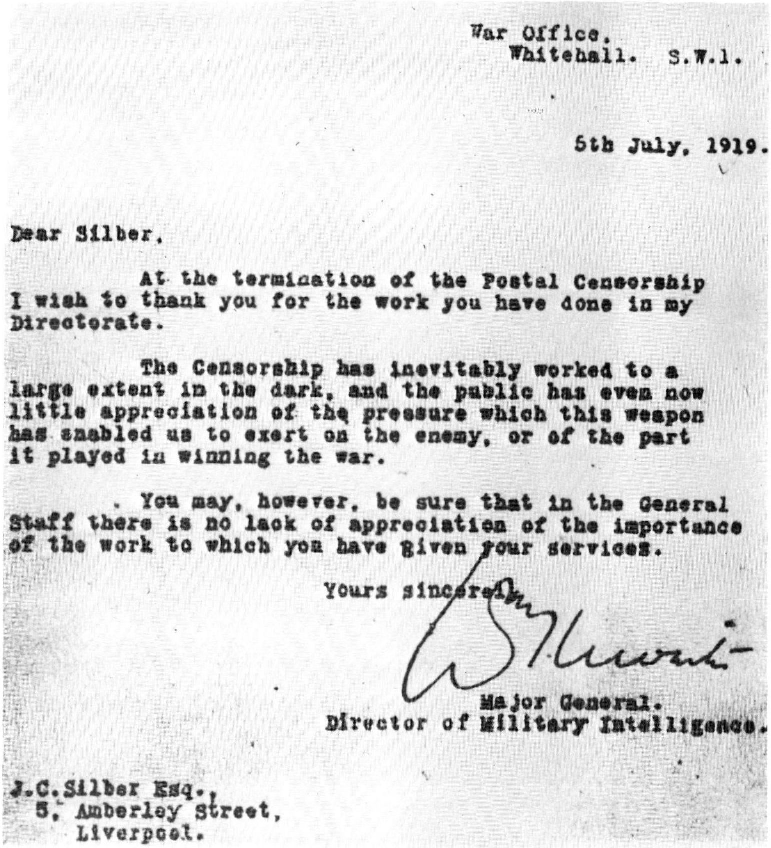

An embarrassing accolade. Jules Silber, the perfect spy, had spent the entire war passing to the Germans information collected at his job in postal censorship.

calling on the girl as an official government censor to warn her of her indiscretion, and in the course of conversation he collected the information he wanted.

The only hazards he ever seems to have encountered were those of promotion and conscription. He refused promotion, which would have taken him out of direct contact with the mail, and he had to take drugs to disguise his good health and enable him to stay where he was. The drugs were effective – he had a complete breakdown at the end of the war. Never suspected, he went on living in England until 1925. He then returned to the Fatherland and wrote a book on his experiences as a German spy. The book proved a very nasty shock to a great many people.

Silber's case is a good illustration of one of the virtually insoluble problems inherent in espionage: the really intelligent and trusted individual who happens to be an enemy spy. The Austrian, Karl Zievert, is another example. He had lived in Russia for nearly all his life, and for more than forty years had been employed by the Ministry of the Interior as a secret postal censor in Kiev. Impregnably established as a loyal servant of the Romanovs, he was also serving the interests of Austria and Germany. He, however, worked for money, drawing one

salary from the Russians, another from the Austrians, and payments from Berlin on a piece-work basis.

Military intelligence in the First World War was confronted by a major problem as soon as mobile operations ended with the first battle of Ypres in October 1914. Both sides then dug lines of trenches from the English Channel to the Alps, producing a tactical situation described by Lord Wavell as 'conditions of siege', in which there were no flanks and no opportunities for spies and couriers to flit to and fro as they had done in the days when James II of England had fought at Arras. It became very difficult to find out what was happening behind the enemy lines. The aeroplane equipped with a camera – usually held by the 'observer' – was one obvious source of information, and the pioneer of aerial photography, Lieutenant J. T. C. Moore-Brabazon (later Lord Brabazon of Tara), has recorded in his book *The Brabazon Story* that

because it didn't seem to be playing the game to take photographs of the enemy lines, Colonel Trenchard [his commanding officer, later Lord Trenchard] used to go about with these photographs in his pocket, trying to make people use them.

The information which intelligence staffs needed most was anything which would give early warning of the build-up before an enemy offensive. This was normally directly related to troop movements, usually by rail, a considerable distance behind the lines.

Three types of source could provide this information: agents on short-term missions, resident agents who lived near railway junctions, and local inhabitants. It was easy enough to obtain; the difficulty lay

Air reconnaissance, 1913: a Royal Flying Corps pilot is briefed for a mission. Traditionalists at first opposed this form of intelligence gathering on the grounds that 'it didn't seem to be playing the game'.

in getting it back across the lines in time for it to be of use. The British devised all sorts of methods.

Aircraft depositing and picking up agents flew over at night, landed, and took off again from moonlit fields, but this extremely hazardous operation, apparently first developed by Bert Hall, a freelance American pilot employed by the Turks in 1912 in their warfare against Bulgars, Serbs and Greeks, was too expensive in men and machines. Agents then strapped themselves into 'Guardian Angel' parachutes, the product of the Inventions Board of the Ministry of Munitions, and jumped out of aeroplanes, but the Germans soon grew suspicious of aircraft droning about behind their lines at night without dropping bombs, and reception committees were arranged. Then free balloons were used. Agents carrying wireless sets supplemented by carrier pigeons drifted silently across the enemy lines when the wind was favourable and, surprisingly enough, many of them landed within a reasonable distance of their destination. Yet there was always the problem of communication.

The wireless sets, mainly because of technical incompetence at the receiving end, were never satisfactory. Pigeons were remarkably swift and accurate, but limited in carrying capacity, and dangerous. The

Air observation: the finned balloon was an advance on the spherical type since it remained comparatively stable.

The Pigeon Service, organized initially by Captain Waley, MC, of the intelligence Corps, was fast and efficient but dangerous in enemy-occupied areas. Germans tended to shoot people with pigeons on sight.

Germans were liable to shoot anyone who had a pigeon in a basket or cage without bothering to ask questions. They had tried, with considerable effect, to seal off the Belgian–Dutch frontier – thereby preventing the movement of agents from occupied France and Belgium into neutral Holland – and had erected an electrified fence of lethal power. Information was passed over it by such methods as knotting a message inside a rubber contraceptive, tucking it into a sliced-open potato, turnip or other root, and tossing it to an agent on the other side, but the message could still take up to a fortnight to go through Holland and England to General Headquarters in France. At length a certain Captain Campbell, a mining engineer in civil life, invented a code which could be applied to any newspaper article or letter on any subject, and through the medium of the newspaper *Landwirt*, circulating in Switzerland, messages from occupied France and Belgium could reach the intelligence staff in France within five days.

Troop movements and train watching, though of great importance in forecasting enemy intentions, were basically local operational intelligence. Long-range espionage could only be carried out by agents who risked their lives in enemy territory far beyond the operational zone. One, the Frenchman Charles Lucieto, penetrated the closely guarded security defences of munitions factories at Mannheim and Essen to bring back details of the German development of artillery shells discharging mustard gas. Another French agent, Waegele, was actually commissioner of field police in German headquarters at various locations such as Charleville and Stenay (in France), and one of his best efforts was to send warning of Ludendorff's final tremendous offensive, planned for 27 May 1918. This was to be launched against General Duchêne's Sixth French Army holding the Chemin-des-Dames feature, overlooking Laon and the plain of Champagne. Unfortunately, like Colquhoun Grant's vital information for Wellington before Waterloo, his message arrived too late. However, as Professor Cruttwell has noted in his *History of the Great War*, ample warning of the impending storm was given, but by an agency reckoned to be too inexperienced to be reliable – American Military Intelligence. Their intelligence assessment was extremely accurate, but Duchêne, prone to respond to the warnings of his allies with a terse '*J'ai dit!*', was almost as difficult as the Hanoverian General Dörnberg in 1815.

Great advances were made in developing and improving the techniques and mechanics of intelligence and counter-intelligence between 1914 and 1918, mainly because war was now, more than ever, a national concern which, by involving the whole population of a belligerent country, enabled the war leaders to call upon all resources of skill in every field. Censorship had exploited with very great success the spy's perpetual problem of communication, and signal intelligence had risen to a position of paramount importance. Stieber's legacy of ruthlessness had been accepted; the disappearance of Alexander Szek, the code clerk, is an indication of the bitter secret war. A great many spies and agents died – by execution, by accident, on the electrified frontier fence in Belgium, and in many other ways – but the prize for ingenious and merciless disposal of an enemy, in the Stieber tradition, should perhaps go to Richard Meinertzhagen.

At the beginning of the war he was the intelligence officer of the British force which attacked Tanga on the coast of German East Africa (now Tanzania). During subsequent operations against the German commander, Count von Lettlow-Vorbeck, he discovered that the enemy spymaster was an Arab, living on the shore of Lake Tanganyika. Meinertzhagen wrote a brief letter to him, thanked him for services rendered, enclosed a sum of money, and sent it by a courier he suspected of being a double agent. As Meinertzhagen had foreseen, the courier took it straight to the German commander. Since nobody really trusts a spy or a spymaster, the unfortunate and entirely loyal Arab was taken out of his hut and shot without being asked for an explanation. The trick was repeated during the Palestine campaign in 1917, when Meinertzhagen was Allenby's intelligence officer. A similar letter and sum of money were sent to a Turkish spymaster whose operations had been very successful, and thus, reacting solely to innate suspicion, the Germans and the Turks were persuaded to destroy their own excellent intelligence organizations in East Africa and Palestine.

Napoleon was not the only one to believe that the spy is a natural traitor.

CHAPTER TWELVE
World War

Having won the War to end War, the British, French and Americans demobilized their forces, reduced their intelligence services to the minimum and, by keeping that minimum extremely short of money, left the field open to the Russians, the Japanese and, in due course, the Germans. The British still felt that intelligence was not 'playing the game'. The attitude of many Americans was summed up in the remark made by the Secretary of State, Henry L. Stimson, in 1929, that 'gentlemen do not read each other's mail'.

He said this to justify closing down the American cryptographic bureau known as the Black Chamber, which had been run by Herbert Yardley with a team of cryptographers. Yardley was one of the protégés of the great Van Deman, who retired from the army in 1929. He was understandably embittered at finding himself suddenly out of work, and wrote a book which he called *The American Black Chamber*. It was a best-seller. Nineteen nations, suddenly discovering the extent to which Yardley had been reading their mail, changed their codes.

Fortunately, Henry Stimson's moral attitude does not seem to have had much influence outside political circles, and William F. Friedman, a civilian employed by the United States Army Signal Corps since 1921, was appointed head of a new Signal Intelligence Service (sis) to take the place of the Black Chamber. In 1935 Major Haskell Allison relieved Friedman as head of the sis while the latter devoted all his time to cryptography, and in 1940 Friedman broke the Japanese 'Purple Code' – a mechanical system – thereby making one of the greatest contributions to American victory in the Pacific. In the same category as this almost incredible feat was the British ability to read German 'high grade' (supposedly unbreakable) ciphers so promptly that intelligence gained from them could be transmitted to commanders in the field in time for them to act on it.

By the end of the First World War, Britain's espionage, military intelligence and signal-cum-cryptographic intelligence services were second to none. Military intelligence, ever decreasing, lingered on until the Army of Occupation was withdrawn from the Rhineland in 1929. MI5 and MI6 remained in being, but on a greatly reduced budget, and in the wave of pacifism that followed the war the familiar British political principle that unpleasant facts, if ignored, will cease to exist, was adopted by the country's leaders. They did not want to know what was happening in Germany; in 1930 the regular intelligence reports on German rearmament, produced for the Committee of Imperial Defence, were 'discontinued, for political reasons'. Intelligence, as a military subject, was not even mentioned in the training programmes at the Royal Military College, Sandhurst, or the Staff College at Camberley, and lack of funds reduced the status of many of the overseas agents to little more than that of sleepers.

In America the Federal Bureau of Investigation (FBI), the only counter-espionage organization, was drastically reduced in manpower, and the whole country, preoccupied with economic depression, became dangerously vulnerable to the agents of an ambitious Japan and a resurgent Germany. Furthermore, the large number of Americans of German stock created another hazard, because among them were some not actively anti-American but certainly pro-German in what they regarded as the next inevitable conflict, when the armies of the Fatherland took revenge for the defeat of 1918.

Hence the case of Hermann Lang, a disciple of the paranoiac Austrian housepainter Adolf Hitler, who intended to complete the unfinished labours of Bismarck and Kaiser Wilhelm II and dominate Europe. Lang was one of the founder members of Hitler's Nazi party, and had taken part in the 'Munich March' of November 1923. Ten years later he was employed at the Norden engineering works on Long Island. Soon after Hitler came to power in 1933 the spies and agents of the Abwehr – first of a number of German intelligence organizations – began operating overseas. One agent, with the cover name of Dr Ranken, got in touch with Lang who was working on the development of a new and very secret bomb-sight for the American air force. Lang handed over copies of all the blueprints, and even went to Germany to check the prototype made from them. He needed no persuasion and asked for no payment – like Jules Silber, he did it for the Fatherland. However, it is said that Marshal Hermann Goering, head of the German Luftwaffe, gave him a 'present' of 10,000 marks.

Lang returned to America. In due course Britain was bombed with the aid of the Norden bomb-sight, and Admiral Wilhelm Canaris, then in charge of the Abwehr, realized there was a possibility that the shooting down of the first German bomber equipped with the American bomb-sight would compromise Lang. He tried to get him back to Germany, but was foiled by an FBI agent who had infiltrated the Abwehr. Lang was arrested in 1941 and sentenced to fourteen years' imprisonment. Released in 1950, he returned to Germany and got a job in a factory in Bavaria.

During the period from 1934 until 1939, Germany spread her espionage net throughout Europe and extended it to cover America. The FBI became spyhunters. In England, MI5 had little difficulty in keeping the Abwehr spies under surveillance, because there had been no real improvement in the standard since the days of 'Tiger Eyes' Schragmuller – who died of spinal tuberculosis in Munich in 1940. The

Codenamed Lucy, Rudolph Roessler operated from Switzerland and provided Stalin with precise details (which he ignored) of the 1941 German invasion.

French seemed to have forgotten the lessons Stieber had taught, and the Italians, trying to adapt to life under the Fascist dictator Benito Mussolini, were too busy spying on each other to pay much attention to events elsewhere. The Italian Foreign Minister, Count Galeazzo Ciano, admitted that though, at the outbreak of the Second World War, he had 'a few' agents scattered about the continent, there were none in Britain. Russia was laying the foundations of what, in wartime, was to become the famous *Rote Kapelle*, or Red Orchestra – the name given by German Intelligence to the Soviet spy rings active in Europe – and were recruiting agents who sent in a flood of information from Vienna, Brussels, Berlin, Paris, Oslo, Madrid and Switzerland. Among them was Rudolph Roessler, who lived in Lucerne and had the code name 'Lucy'. He was in contact with a member of Hitler's staff who passed him details of practically every undertaking planned by the German High Command – including the date, time, place and strength of the German invasion of Russia in 1941, which Stalin ignored.

Czech Intelligence, superbly organized by General Frantisek Moravec, was also very active in the face of German threats to 'come to the aid' of the German minority in the Czech population. Guessing that the soldierly bearing of many of his military intelligence agents would arouse suspicion, Moravec issued them with walking-sticks and was

gratified to note that they soon developed a 'civilian slouch'. He also
had the idea of opening small banks in border towns. These specialized
in personal loans, and advertised their services widely in Germany.
German officers, using them to satisfy troublesome creditors, were
allowed to become deeply involved. Selected officers were then
approached by Czech Intelligence, and told of a way in which the bank
loan could be paid off without money.

Genghis Khan's principle of recruiting spies among enemy nationals
had become a standard practice in international espionage, now even
more closely associated with treachery. The main functions of secret
services in the peace following the First World War were to recruit
willing agents and plant sleepers who would wake when the coming
war began.

Even though the Germans were unwilling to acknowledge Stieber's
contribution to intelligence, they were prepared to apply his methods.
Walter Schellenberg, in charge of the section of AMT VI which dealt
with counter-espionage, was responsible for an establishment in Berlin
known as the Salon Kitty, staffed by what he claimed were the most
beautiful and accommodating whores in Europe. Possibly not quite so
depraved as the Green House, it was functionally more efficient, from
the blackmailer's point of view, because it was equipped with concealed
microphones, recording machines and photographic apparatus not
available in Stieber's time. It is said that Count Ciano featured in some
interesting tapes and pictures.

Though considerable advances had been made in technology, the
basic principles and problems of intelligence remained unchanged.
One particular problem, by no means new, seemed to be recurring
more frequently, and it was one to which there is no easy solution. It
concerned the agent's life style or behaviour pattern which, if suddenly
changed, is likely to arouse suspicion. Moravec tells the story of a German colonel, one of his agents, who disregarded many warnings of the
danger of being seen to have more money than his salary warranted.

Salon Kitty, a high-class
brothel organized by the
Nazi counter-espionage
department.

Dusko Popov, seen here with his wife, has claimed that he gave warning of the Japanese Pearl Harbor attack to J. Edgar Hoover *Opposite*, the long-standing head of the FBI. Reasons of temperament may have underlain Hoover's refusal to believe him.

The colonel lost his head, literally, and Moravec lost a very valuable source of information. To the spymaster, the waste of good spies for this reason is infuriating, but it reveals a lack of professionalism or a character weakness in the spy himself which might put more than his own life at risk.

Another eternal problem is that of credibility. The history of intelligence is also the story of a succession of missed opportunities and avoidable disasters: the French did not believe their military attaché in Berlin in 1870; the British ignored the warnings of their own military intelligence before the Boer War; the Russians, too, seem to have been more sceptical than most nations. Their *Rote Kapelle* in Germany, headed by the 'Big Chief' Leopold Trepper, a Polish Jew, became a nightmare to Admiral Canaris and Reichsführer Heinrich Himmler, the heads of the two main intelligence services. Even Hitler, in 1942, admitted the superiority of Russian espionage, yet much of its detailed and accurate information, particularly on Germany's intentions towards Russia, was merely filed.

The Yugoslavian spy, Dusko Popov, in his recent book *Spy, Counterspy*, claims that he gave details of the proposed Japanese attack on Pearl Harbor to J. Edgar Hoover, head of the FBI, well in advance, and that nothing was done. There is no doubt that Hoover was a difficult man whose years in authority had made him intolerant and may have led him to believe that he was infallible. He seems to have taken a personal dislike to the plausible Popov, who apparently knew so much more than he did, but the events leading up to the attack are a separate study in itself.

It is one of the lessons to be learned from intelligence history that the spy, no matter how good he is, will seldom make any headway against the prejudice of his masters, a prejudice normally compounded,

in varying quantities, of innate distrust, preconceived ideas, and fear of being deceived by the enemy who may be feeding false information to the spy. Considerable strength of character is needed to overcome the common human fault of believing only what one wants to believe.

The Second World War grew out of the Great War of 1914–18 but, apart from the initial *Blitzkrieg*, it bore little resemblance to either von Moltke's swift campaign in 1870 or the slaughter in the trenches. In their secret world spies went about their business much as they had done for the past twenty years and, as more money became available, spymasters were able to increase the size of their services. Since war always stimulates the invention of new ways of destroying the enemy, highly sophisticated communications, miniature photographic equipment, and silent lethal weapons were developed for use by spies. It became possible to reduce a foolscap page of information to the size of a small punctuation mark – the microdot – and ingenious hiding-places for information, on paper or film, rivalled those of the spies and couriers in the Peninsular War. Yet, so far as the human element was concerned, nothing had changed since the days of Joshua.

One of the principal features of espionage in the Second World War was the failure of the Germans ever to produce a really effective and reliable secret service, and this was because they ignored the fundamental principle of centralization. Himmler ran his own *Sicherheitsdienst* (SD) which contained the intelligence and counter-intelligence branches of the *Schutzstaffel* (SS), later sub-divided into sections such as AMT VI, SIPO and the Gestapo. These were nominally under the control of the main security office. Quite separate was the Abwehr of Wilhelm Canaris. Himmler was a ruthless, brutal and dedicated Nazi. Canaris was not. Indeed, his attitude to Nazism has since led many people to believe, erroneously, that he was a British agent. Between two such men there was no common ground.

The defection to the British in 1944 of Dr Vermehren, the Abwehr agent in Ankara whose wife, Countess Plettenberg, was Catholic and anti-Nazi, gave Himmler the opportunity he had long awaited. Canaris was first dismissed and then arrested, and the Abwehr was incorporated into the Gestapo. On 8 April 1945, exactly one month before Germany's unconditional surrender, Canaris was taken out, naked, into the execution yard of Flossenberg prison and slowly hanged twice, with piano wire, for the amusement of Himmler's Gestapo butchers.

Naturally the existence of two separate intelligence services, the proliferation of other agencies, and the enmity of spymasters, prevented any efficient co-ordination of the German system. Although the Germans did have two reasonably competent agents in Britain – the Welsh nationalist Arthur Owens, and Alfred Wahring – many were of the standard of the unfortunate Karel Richter. He was dropped by parachute near St Albans on a summer night, and when picked up – largely as the result of bad luck – was unable to explain why he was wearing three sets of underclothes and two pairs of socks. The Abwehr con-

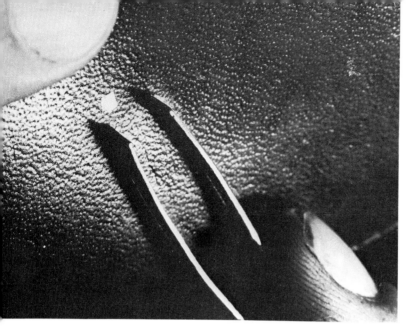

The microdot – a page of information reduced to a punctuation mark. Espionage has been a beneficiary of developments in twentieth-century technology.

stantly repeated the mistake of using spies who had little or no knowledge of local conditions, geography and customs, and only a poor understanding of the language. Lord Jowitt, who prosecuted some of them, said that only one could speak English reasonably fluently. Stieber would have been shocked.

Ever since the invention of the electric telegraph, signal intelligence had proved to be of supreme importance because an ability to read the enemy's messages while they are in transit means that the interceptor knows what the enemy proposes to do before he actually does it. This was the reason why the American SIS devoted much time to cryptography between the wars, and why one of the British MI6 intelligence tasks during the same period was to obtain details of any codes or secret systems likely to be used by potential enemies, such as Germany.

The British acquired the secrets of the German 'Enigma' machine – which turned a message into an unintelligible scramble before transmitting it in Morse – from an anti-German Pole working in the German factory which built the machines, some time before the war. When the war began, a number of wireless operators, cryptographers and intelligence officers formed a special team at what was called Station X at Bletchley Park, a Victorian mansion in Buckinghamshire. Station X brought off a large number of extraordinary intelligence *coups*.

One was the breaking of the German U-boat code, with the result that the Royal Navy was able to hunt, find and sink German submarines at a rate faster than they could be replaced. Another was the reading of Field-Marshal Rommel's message to Field-Marshal Kesselring describing a trap laid for the victorious Eighth Army during the pursuit after the battle of Alamein. Knowing his enemy's intentions, General Montgomery was able to turn to his own advantage events which might have been disastrous. Yet, as the Americans were to find, information of this sort, and of this grade of secrecy, creates its own problems. If the source of information is kept secret, and if the information appears to be far removed from the intelligence assessments of commanders in the field, it will not be believed. This happened in Crete. When Crete was lost, Winston Churchill ordered an inquiry, and the result was a report which stated there need have been no defeat if commanders had believed and acted on the information Station X had supplied. Thereafter, commanders and their chiefs of staff at certain levels were told when intelligence had come from monitored signals traffic and were able to attach due weight to it.

The other major problem is best illustrated by the story of the shooting down of Admiral Isoroku Yamamoto, Commander-in-Chief of the Japanese navy. The Americans intercepted a message which gave exact details of the Admiral's tour of Japanese units in China, Truk and Bougainville, and which stated that he and his staff would be travelling in two Mitsubishi bombers with an escort of six Zero fighters. Two groups of American Lightning fighters laid an ambush and dealt very competently with all the Japanese aircraft. It then became absolutely essential to conceal all American knowledge of what had happened to Yamamoto. For if the Japanese realized that the loss, which they could ill afford, was not the result of a chance encounter, they would know the Americans had broken the Purple Code which they considered to be indecipherable (to anyone but a man like Friedman, it probably was) and would change it. There were several scares – one being a report filed by a war correspondent unaware of its implications. Fortunately it was 'killed' by a naval censor, and the Japanese ascribed the loss of their admiral to the fortunes of war. This underlines the supreme importance, in espionage, of preventing the enemy from finding out how much you know. Neither the Japanese nor the Germans ever discovered that the enemy was 'reading their mail'.

The American SIS also had its great successes which, like the British interception of Rommel's message to Kesselring, completely changed a tactical situation. One of them concerned the Japanese proposed invasion of Midway. In the spring of 1942 the Americans learned of Japanese plans for a major attack on a target described in their signals as 'AF', which could have been Midway, Hawaii or the Aleutians. Admiral Chester Nimitz suspected the target was Midway. He therefore ordered the Midway garrison commander to radio Pearl Harbor in clear that his water supply was dangerously low. Three days later, patient listeners and cryptographers received a Japanese report of a shortage of water at 'AF'. So when the Japanese attacked, with all the confidence gained from their success at Pearl Harbor, they found that this time the Americans were waiting for them. Their shattering defeat was the turning point of the war in the Pacific.

Among the outstanding spies of the Second World War were the German Richard Sorge, an ardent Communist and professional spy for Russia; Takeo Yoshikawa, the Japanese naval intelligence officer who made all the preparations for the raid on Pearl Harbor; 'George Wood', the genuine ideologist in the German Foreign Office; Elyesa Bazna,

William F. Friedman, whose 'breaking' of the Japanese Purple Code contributed greatly to American victory in the Pacific.

otherwise known as 'Cicero', the Turkish amateur who worked for himself; and a Frenchman named René Duchez, another amateur but an opportunist of rare quality and courage.

Several books have been written about Sorge, the brilliant journalist who became *persona* very much *grata* in the German embassy in Japan, and ran a spy ring which penetrated the Japanese War Cabinet. He, like the *Rote Kapelle* and Rudolf Roessler, gave Stalin details of German invasion plans in 1941. He also answered Russia's most vital question – whether the Japanese would launch their main effort against eastern Russia or go south, into the Pacific. When he knew were going south, Stalin was able to deploy against the Germans the divisions he had been holding to counter the Japanese threat. Sorge was caught, tried and hanged by the Japanese on the wooden gallows in Sugamo prison on 7 November 1944. Almost to the end he believed Stalin would make some attempt to save him, but the Russian dictator took little interest in the lives or safety of those who served him.

Hanako-san, Sorge's faithful Japanese mistress, eventually found his grave in Tokyo. From the gold fillings in his teeth she made a ring which she wore in memory of him, thus giving the lie to all the legends that he was not executed and even managed to murder a girl said to

Apotheosis of a superspy: Richard Sorge, whose brilliant work in Japan enabled Stalin to release the Soviets' Siberian army against the German invasion in the west. With the sculpture is Hanako-san, Sorge's devoted mistress. On her finger is a ring made from Sorge's gold tooth fillings, taken after his execution.

have betrayed him. Not until after the death of Stalin – who, to conceal his own shortcomings, had tried to make out that Sorge was a double agent and therefore unreliable – was he properly acknowledged as one of the greatest spies of the twentieth century. In 1964, twenty years after his execution, he was made a Hero of the Soviet Union, a street in Moscow was named after him, and his portrait, reproduced from a 1937 passport, appeared on a postage stamp.

Takeo Yoshikawa, discharged from the Japanese navy as unfit, arrived in Hawaii in the spring of 1941 and was attached to the embassy staff. He made contact with a Nazi agent, Dr Friedel Kühn, formerly an *Oberleutnant* of the German navy, whose cover was that of an anti-Nazi scholar with a considerable private income, studying the roots of the Japanese language. Kühn had brought his family with him, a wife and two step-children, and his step-daughter Ruth was well equipped to play the part of the beautiful spy. She opened a beauty parlour catering for the needs, and indiscretions, of the wives of American naval officers. This little spy ring, led by Yoshikawa, prepared the way for the devastating Japanese surprise attack just before eight o'clock on the morning of Sunday, 7 December 1941. The Kühn family was arrested within an hour of the raid, and Kühn was sentenced to fifty years in Alcatraz, though his family was allowed to return to Germany. Yoshikawa was interned as an enemy vice-consul and sent back to Japan as part of an ordinary diplomatic exchange during the following year. His secret role was not discovered. He spent the rest of the war in Japanese Naval Intelligence.

'George Wood' was the cover name for a member of the German Foreign Office who appeared in Switzerland in August 1943 and handed a mass of information over to American Intelligence – more than 2,700 documents during a period of time, some of which 'blew' the Turkish spy, Cicero, in Ankara. 'George Wood' was another Jules Silber in that he had no thought of reward, but, unlike Silber, he was not working for the Fatherland. He was a complete amateur of remarkable courage, whose sole wish was to see the destruction of Nazism.

Sorge, Yoshikawa, the Kühns and 'George Wood' were all ideologists, dedicated to a cause. Elyesa Bazna – Cicero – worked only for money, like so many spies, and he is a classic example of the spy who produces information so revealing and so valuable that it is at once regarded as a trap. Perhaps if Sir Hughe Knatchbull-Hugessen had been a little more security-minded, Cicero would never have been anything more than one of the domestic servants employed in the embassy. As it was, searching for secrets to sell, he became the ambassador's valet, took impressions of his keys, and at every convenient moment photographed the documents which his master was careless enough to bring up from his office and leave in his bedroom safe for leisurely perusal. Through a contact in the German embassy named Moyzisch, the photographed information reached Ribbentrop, the German Foreign Minister. But Ribbentrop refused to believe that a servant could have access to such things as the list of British agents in Turkey, details of matters discussed at Allied conferences, plans for the invasion of Europe, and the key to the diplomatic code. He told Franz von Papen, then German ambassador in Ankara, that it was all much too good to be true. Von Papen and his staff had no doubt whatsoever about Cicero's genuineness, and Moyzisch was sent to try and convince Kaltenbrunner, who was in charge of the main security office. Kaltenbrunner remained sceptical, but he made £200,000 available in English notes to pay for the exploitation of Cicero. Ribbentrop, however, resolutely declined to act on any of the information passed to him from this source.

When 'George Wood' told the Americans in Switzerland about Cicero, they investigated. Moyzisch got wind of their inquiries and warned Bazna, who swiftly gathered up his store of British banknotes – said to have been about £300,000 – which he kept under the carpet in his room, and disappeared. Later he discovered that every note he had been given by the Germans was counterfeit and came from the vast quantity printed in Berlin as part of a plan to debase British currency.

René Duchez was a housepainter, and while ostensibly negotiating a contract for redecorating rooms in the German headquarters in Caen he took the top secret blueprints of the Atlantic Wall – the German-built coastal defences of France – from a file on the desk of Colonel Hugo Schnedderer, the local commandant, while the colonel turned away to speak to someone in an adjoining room. Duchez hid the maps immediately, behind a picture in the commandant's office, and retrieved them when he returned to paint the room. He was suspected and followed to a café by Gestapo men, who searched him but found nothing. Duchez had hidden the package in an army greatcoat hanging against the wall, while the German soldier who owned it was sitting at a table with a French girl. The maps reached London by way of a French fishing boat and an English trawler.

Many books on espionage written since the Second World War give considerable space either to the British 'Special Operations Executive' (SOE) or to the American 'Office of Strategic Services' (OSS), telling the stories of Odette Sansom, Yeo Thomas and Peter Churchill, Christine Granville alias Jacqueline Armand, Violette Szabo, and Noor Inayat Khan of SOE. The Americans write of Major-General 'Wild Bill' Donovan, John Shaheen and Carl Eiffler. Yet the primary functions of these organizations were sabotage and subversion. Those who belonged to them set out to organize resistance and cause discomfort, distress and despair to the enemy on the largest possible scale. Many died. Many suffered abominable tortures at the hands of the Gestapo and the Japanese equivalent, the Kempeitai. All were brave to the point of foolhardiness, but their missions were operational and not primarily intelligence; any information gained was often a bonus, but the difficulties of transmitting it were sometimes insuperable.

Germany, too, had her gladiators in this contest of private armies, in particular the huge scar-faced Austrian, Otto Skorzeny, who kidnapped Admiral Nicholas Horthy, dictator of Hungary, before he fell into the hands of advancing Russian troops. Skorzeny, in a small plane, also snatched Benito Mussolini from a mountain top where he was held by 300 Italian guards.

Deception has often played a notable part in operational planning and preparation, and it is an aspect of intelligence work at which the British have long been peculiarly adept. There are many examples: Lord Allenby won the second battle of Gaza in the autumn of 1917 largely because of a blood-stained haversack dropped by Richard Meinertzhagen in front of a Turkish patrol as he galloped away, pretending to be wounded. The haversack contained convincing documents which induced the Turks to change their defensive positions. In the Second World War two of the best illustrations of this art relate to the invasion of Sicily and the assault on Hitler's Atlantic Wall.

At the end of April 1943 the drowned body of Major William Martin, Royal Marines, was washed ashore near Huelva in the Gulf of Cadiz, with a brief-case containing sealed envelopes chained to the wrist. Not far away floated a small rubber dinghy – obviously from a ditched aircraft. The pockets of the dead man's uniform contained details of a sad little story. Apart from Identity Card No. 148228 there was a worn photograph of a girl and letters signed 'Pam', a jeweller's receipt for an engagement ring, ticket stubs from a London theatre, bus tickets, keys, and a gentle letter from a bank manager about a slight overdraft. The Spaniards carried out a post mortem, and the presence of water in the lungs confirmed that death had been by drowning. Since the sympathies of the Chief of the Spanish Naval Staff lay with Hitler there was a delay of two weeks before the brief-case was handed over to the British ambassador, and in that time the contents had been copied and the envelopes carefully resealed by a German agent. They revealed that the awaited invasion of southern Europe would not be in Sicily, as expected, but in Sardinia, with diversionary attacks in Greece.

Also during this delay there had been an urgent exchange of signals between British high commands on the whereabouts of papers of great secrecy and importance known to have been in the possession of a courier named Major Martin.

It does not seem to have entered the minds of German commanders such as Admiral Doenitz and Field-Marshals Keitel and Rommel that the whole thing might be a plant. The corpse was that of an unnamed civilian who had died in London of pneumonia – hence the water in the lungs – and been taken to the Spanish coast by submarine. The rest of the evidence had been contrived. The Germans regarded the drowning of Major Martin as an extraordinary piece of luck and carried out a major redistribution of land, sea and air forces to meet the attacks in Sardinia and Greece. On 10 July the Allies landed in Sicily.

The deceptive measures designed to convince Hitler that the main Allied attack on the 'Fortress of Europe' was going to be in the area of the Pas de Calais would fill a whole book, but among them was one which convinced the Germans that although tension was rising there was no immediate likelihood of attack. General Montgomery, known to be one of the principal commanders of the invasion forces, was making leisurely visits to British troops in Gibraltar and North Africa with the usual team of war correspondents and press photographers. In fact, this 'General Montgomery' was an actor named M. E. Clifton-James, commissioned into the Royal Army Pay Corps, who bore so striking a resemblance to the General as to deceive most people. It was not a new idea. There were many occasions in the Middle Ages when mailed and visored knights rode into battle bearing someone else's shield in order to confuse the enemy or draw their attention away from a king or commander.

Throughout the war, women in many countries were employed in every branch of intelligence. In the United Kingdom some became photographic interpreters – especially in the team which unravelled the secrets of Peenemunde and the development of German pilotless aircraft (V-1s) and rockets (V-2s). Others worked in Room 39 of the Admiralty (successor of Blinker Hall's Room 40), at Bletchley, and in the intelligence staffs of the War Office and the Air Ministry. They

A secretly taken photograph of a V-2 rocket being launched from Peenemunde, September 1944.

were collectors, collators, analysts, evaluators, interpreters and couriers. They served on recruiting and training staffs. On counter-intelligence staffs they handled censorship and movement control. They were ubiquitous and invaluable, and in view of their great contribution to their national intelligence services it is perhaps of interest to recall the remarks made about women in intelligence by Colonel David Henderson in the first official British intelligence manual, published in April 1904:

When women are employed as secret service agents, the probability of success and the difficulty of administration are alike increased. Women are frequently very skilful at eliciting information; they require no disguise; if attractive they are likely to be welcome everywhere, and may be able to seduce from their loyalty those whose assistance or indiscretion may be of use. On the other hand, they are variable, easily offended, seldom sufficiently reticent, and apt to be reckless. Their treatment requires the most watchful discretion. Usually they will work more consistently for a person than for a principle, and a lover in the Intelligence Corps makes a useful intermediary.

Apart from trained agents and all those who worked in the organization and administration of intelligence, hundreds of people were employed by espionage agents as observers and informants, sometimes without realizing the use to which their information was being put. Agents are wont to look for this type of recruit among professions and occupations which involve frequent casual contact with a cross-section of society, and many prostitutes, barmaids, hotel domestic staff and receptionists employed by commercial and other organizations found opportunities to increase their earnings with little apparent effort or risk.

Some women took great risks, but on the whole they were far better trained and more professional than their counterparts in the First World War. Yet intelligence is not, nor can it ever be, an exact science. Time and time again the fate of a spy has depended on some chance, incident or coincidence which could not possibly have been foreseen and had nothing to do with training or experience. The training of a spy can do no more than deal with principles and pitfalls. It can outline the most sensible course to adopt within given circumstances. It can, for example, indicate ways of 'losing a shadow' – evading a follower – or the technicalities of eavesdropping, but it cannot provide for every contingency. In the end a spy is nearly always on his or her own in a lonely, dangerous world, where survival and success may depend entirely on exploiting a sudden opportunity with courage and swiftness of reaction.

CHAPTER THIRTEEN

Cold War

Adolf Hitler committed suicide on 1 May 1945. Six days later, Germany surrendered. In the Far East, after the dropping of atomic bombs on Hiroshima and Nagasaki, the Japanese capitulated on 14 August 1945. All over the world, except in Russia and China, millions of sailors, soldiers and airmen went home rejoicing and took off their uniforms. Russia, under Josef Stalin, lost no time in engulfing Poland, Rumania, Bulgaria, Hungary, East Germany and Czechoslovakia. In China, Mao Tse-tung defeated the armies of the Kuomintang, and the Land of the Peacock Throne became a Communist state. Western empires dissolved, the 'Iron Curtain' came down, and the world divided in a straightforward contest between the relative freedom of democracy and what Solzhenitsyn has described as the slavery of Communism.

Amidst a turmoil of changing values and social upheaval throughout the world there was one dominant military and political factor: the atomic bomb, regarded as not only the ultimate weapon but also the ultimate deterrent. Purely as a threat, it was the bulwark of the Western Powers against the imposition of international Communism by armed force; and naturally, since Russia did not possess the secrets of its manufacture, it was Russia's major espionage target. There was to be no rest for secret agents who had risked their lives during the shooting war, for they were now involved in a cold war between vastly different ideologies. Yet, unrealized by many of them, espionage – and intelligence – had entered a new phase.

Hitherto it had been the practice in many countries to train agents and despatch them on their tasks as individuals, in the belief that an agent working more or less alone runs fewer risks. Except in the case of Russia, the base organization usually operated with as small a staff as possible, on the principle that the fewer 'in the know' the safer the agents. This system began to change during the Second World War, particularly when espionage and 'special operations' became intermingled, and one of the results of the war was the emergence of the superpowers, America and Russia, both advocates of large bureaucratic institutions. Secret services – though long established in Russia – now became institutions in the Western democracies to a far greater extent than ever before, particularly in America. Spies became civil servants, directed by spymasters such as Lavrenti Beria in Russia and Allen Dulles in America.

America had been slow to develop her intelligence resources. The first United States secret service, officially established in 1865, had nothing to do with espionage; its function was to suppress forgery and counterfeiting. It moved into the world of counter-espionage during the Spanish-American War of 1898, and after the assassination of President McKinley in 1901 it took on responsibility for the personal safety of the President and his family. Then, in 1907, the Federal Bureau of Investigation came into being as an investigating agency with federal powers under the Department of Justice. The functions of the two departments overlapped; in the First World War the FBI undertook security and counter-espionage, eclipsing the secret service which reverted to its original role. At the time of the Japanese attack on Pearl Harbor there was still no central intelligence organization. J. Edgar Hoover, head of the FBI, devoted most of the energies of his department to spy-catching, and warnings of Japanese intentions were not properly collated and evaluated. After the disaster at Pearl Harbor it was realized – in high government circles, for the first time – that the activities and reports of spies and agents, no matter how timely and accurate, count for nothing if there are no experts to process them and bring them to the notice of the proper authority.

To fill this gap the Office of Strategic Services (OSS) was founded by General William J. Donovan in 1942, to collect information and intelligence and send agents into enemy country. As early as 1944 he suggested there should be a central agency with dual functions similar to those of the British MI5 and MI6, but not until September 1947, twenty-one months after President Truman had disbanded the OSS (in January 1946), did the Central Intelligence Agency, the CIA, come into existence. Allen Dulles, one of its originators and a member of the OSS during the war, proposed that it should be an autonomous organization, responsible for its own personnel and for all intelligence operations; only the CIA should be able to make contact with similar agencies of other countries, and the director should be a civilian. In the latter he was overruled, for Admiral Hillenkoetter was appointed.

Formed under the National Security Act, the CIA had wide powers not merely to centralize intelligence but 'to perform such other functions and duties related to intelligence affecting the national security as the National Security Council may from time to time direct'. Dulles maintained that these powers would not be abused so long as the CIA confined itself to facts and did not intrude into policy. It seems this restriction was not always observed, least of all by Dulles himself when he became director in 1953. At this time, John Foster Dulles was Secretary of State in the Eisenhower administration, and the authority exercised by the two brothers was considerable. Nevertheless, the principle behind the CIA was the fundamental intelligence one of centralization; for all its faults and alleged excesses the CIA was essential as an effective counter to Russian Intelligence.

Under Allen Dulles, who has been called the greatest spymaster of his age, the CIA became the most powerful intelligence agency in the

Opposite, Allen Dulles, director of the CIA 1953–61. Undeniably a great spymaster, he has been criticized on the grounds that he exceeded his mandate by interfering in the internal affairs of other countries.

world and, in his own words, 'a tightly knit and efficient spy-shop'. He stated with some pride that the Act of 1947 had 'given Intelligence a more influential position in our Government than Intelligence enjoys in any other government in the world', but President Truman claimed that the CIA conducted its own foreign policy and interfered in the internal affairs of other nations.

Nevertheless, alarm at the power acquired by a national intelligence organization has not been confined to America. In Russia under Stalin, the MVD (as it was then called) with at its head the unscrupulous Lavrenti Beria, Stalin's last chief of police, had been built up into an enormous, ruthless apparatus answerable only to Stalin himself. When Stalin died in 1953 his successors, genuinely afraid of Beria's personal power, moved swiftly to deal with it. Beria had too many enemies and too few friends to be able to survive. He was arrested and executed. The MVD was downgraded from a ministry to a state committee, renamed the KGB, and placed under the control of the Party and the Politburo in the charge of a career bureaucrat, Yuri Andropov – who was not even a full member of the Politburo until 1974.

The CIA was undoubtedly more powerful politically than the KGB, but far smaller. In 1969 the published figure of CIA personnel was 142,000; it has since been reduced to 80,000. Andropov, from his office in the building on Moscow's Dzerzhinsky Square, which also contains Lubyanka prison, controls an 'army' 500,000 strong. It includes nearly 100,000 staff officers of military rank, but does not include the large units of uniformed KGB border guards and an incalculable number of part-time spies and informants all over the world. The KGB and its military counterpart, the GRU, operate a vast network of espionage, largely through Soviet embassies, since a high percentage of Soviet diplomats are trained intelligence officers.

The USA and the USSR have a not dissimilar ideological background, since both evolved from revolution inspired initially by a desire to throw off the 'yoke of the oppressor', but while one nation still preaches freedom and democracy, the other remains a police state exercising absolute control over its people. America hopes to preserve a defensive freedom, while Russia is pledged to an aggressive ideological imperialism. There is perhaps a touch of irony in the fact that the defensive freedom-lovers have developed an aggressive espionage system, which has in the past exerted a direct operational influence on the domestic affairs of countries posing a threat to Western democracy.

The aggressive imperialists, on the other hand, have a system subjected to rigorous bureaucratic control in which a large proportion of effort is devoted to the collection of information – although the KGB is primarily an instrument of repression. The 2nd and 5th Directorates of the KGB deal with all forms of political dissent, the monitoring of communications, censorship, keeping track of all foreigners in the country, and in general maintaining a very tight grip on the internal security of the Soviet Union. Its 1st Directorage (there is no 3rd or 4th) handles all 'foreign operations' using embassy staffs, illegal *'rezidents'* in target countries, and local agents or spies who are nationals of those countries.

The 'foreign operations' on both sides have been extensive. The peak American period was during Dulles's tenure of office from 1953 to 1961, and major coups included the overthrow of Mossadeq in Iran and Arbenz in Guatemala, involvement in the revolt of the Generals in Algeria, machinations in the Congo, the over-flying of Soviet territory by U-2 'spy planes', and the building of the famous Berlin Tunnel to tap an underground telephone exchange in the village of Alt Glienicke, 600 yards from the American Sector. Finally Dulles mounted an air and sea invasion of Cuba to bring down Fidel Castro, using *émigré* Cubans, but the total failure of the 'Bay of Pigs' operation seemed to justify accusations that the CIA was exceeding its powers. Dulles and his assistant, Richard Bissell, resigned. Since then the influence of the CIA has been felt in Chile, the Dominican Republic and elsewhere.

Russia has been 'interfering' in the affairs of other countries for far longer than America – providing funds for local Communist parties, supporting guerrillas and terrorists, and taking an active interest in coups and revolutions in many parts of the world. The KGB was involved in the plots against President Sadat of Egypt and General Numeiry of the Sudan, and it has done its best to encourage anti-Tito groups. To it can be attributed the long war and final result in Angola, much of the trouble in South America, and rebellion in the Persian Gulf. Weapons used by the Irish Republican Army have been traced back to Moscow. Moreover, the KGB will wage war on individuals, in the cause of 'decomposition'. In the mid-1960s great efforts were made in Moscow to compromise Maurice Dejean, the French ambassador, and employ the usual weapons of seduction and blackmail to force him to become a Russian agent in close contact with President Charles de Gaulle. The plans of the KGB failed, but Dejean's career was ruined. At this time a certain Commander Anthony Courtney, the Member for Harrow, asked a number of questions and spoke at some length in the House of Commons about the unnecessarily large number of 'staff' in the Soviety embassy in London, known to be the centre of a large espionage organization operating in the United Kingdom. His activities so irked the Russians that they mounted a deliberate, carefully planned 'decomposition' operation against him – with the result that his parliamentary career was ruined and he could speak no more in the House. In the end they achieved nothing and the Commander's reputation need not have been destroyed, because in 1971 the defector Oleg Lyalin named 105 Soviet agents working in Britain. They were all expelled and the cuts in the Soviet embassy establishment, which Commander Courtney had called for, came about automatically.

Both the CIA and the KGB have their problems. The CIA is bedevilled by adverse publicity, which is vastly damaging and would never be tolerated in Russia. Many Americans seem to be almost masochistic in their apparent determination to destroy their own intelligence

Reinhard Gehlen, the German spymaster and expert on Soviet affairs who turned his espionage network over to the Americans at the end of the Second World War.

organization which, however much they may denigrate it, may be one of the few remaining defences against international Communism. The KGB suffers from faults which are the legacy of Russian history, because in a police state permeated with spies no one trusts anyone and individual initiative is discouraged if not punished. The Russian spy works to explicit instructions and is reluctant to deviate from them, despite changes in circumstances. Even an agent as senior and as competent as Colonel Abel in New York appears to have had no say in the selection of other Russians sent to join his spy ring. Departmental influence and bureaucratic inflexibility have had disastrous results.

The British, although they have a long history of secret services and espionage, have only comparatively recently accepted the need to centralize within a high-level committee: the Security Service (MI5) is under the Home Office; MI6 is the responsibility of the Foreign Office; and service intelligence is controlled by the Defence Intelligence Staff in the Ministry of Defence.

In France under de Gaulle's presidency there was a proliferation of intelligence agencies, because de Gaulle himself would not allow any concentration of power in a single security service; and since he was faced more than once with serious threats of civil war, his reasons were sound. However, under President Valery Giscard d'Estaing the SDECE (service of external documentation and counter-espionage), the 2,000-strong equivalent of the CIA – known as the 'Swimming-pool' because its headquarters is close to the Tourelles swimming-pool just outside Paris – has become highly professional. Though chiefly concerned with operations abroad, and the protection of French interests against the growth of Soviet and Communist influences, the SDECE also deals with internal security.

The West German system owes its inception to an agent who was also a spymaster – General Reinhard Gehlen who, during the Second World War, had been in charge of the Foreign Armies East Section of German Military Intelligence, and had become an expert on the Soviet Union. As soon as he realized the defeat of Germany was inevitable, Gehlen told his network of spies in Eastern Europe to lie low; then, as the Americans advanced through Bavaria, he offered his services and those of his organization to them. In 1955 he became the head of the Federal Intelligence Service for the new West German Republic, and though his large and efficient anti-Communist organization suffered every now and again from penetration by Communist double agents, it collected a great deal of information from the other side of the Iron Curtain.

The Russian attempt to fill the gaps left by the Americans after the Vietnam war has, naturally enough, diverted the attention of Chinese Intelligence from America to Russia. The Chinese are, and have been for thousands of years, a secretive people, addicted to secret societies, and very little is known of their intelligence operations. When Liao Ho-shu, Chinese Chargé d'affaires at The Hague, defected in 1969, he was described as a 'master spy' but, soon discovering he was only a middle-aged diplomat with an emotional problem, the CIA helped him to return to China. There are certain well-defined differences between Chinese Intelligence and that of either of the superpowers. In the first place, Chinese all over the world have a stronger sentimental attachment to the 'homeland' – although they may never have been there – than that of any other nation, including the Russians. They remain Chinese and rarely, even after many years, adopt another culture. The recruiting of agents is thus no problem, and since the Chinese are ubiquitous, the spread and scope of the Chinese intelligence potential is incalculable. Secondly, the Chinese have unlimited patience in building espionage networks and, rather than pay an agent, or use Soviet methods of blackmail and coercion, they will concentrate on 'ideological sympathy'. It has been said that the Chinese have to do this because they do not have the resources of the KGB or the CIA, but there is no doubt that Chinese agents are far more politically motivated than those of other powers.

Thirdly, though not averse to 'dirty tricks', they are less prone to bribing, blackmailing and violence than the superpowers, and their espionage depends more on the careful collection and analysis of material from reasonably overt sources. Moreover, it tends to be defensive rather than offensive; the West is not their target, they want to see Western Europe as strong and united as possible, to counter the Soviet threat. Thus the operations they do undertake are usually designed to show up Soviet intentions in their ideological struggle against Russian Communism.

All espionage systems, no matter how carefully controlled and directed, share a common, fundamental weakness: their security is largely dependent on the loyalty of the individuals who work for them. They are at the mercy of the defector.

Defection is seldom a spontaneous act. Very often it is the escape to comparative safety of an agent who has been operating for some time, and who realizes that secret police or counter-espionage agents are getting too close; yet the first notable post-war defector does seem to have acted on the spur of the moment. He was Igor Gouzenko, serving under Colonel Nikolai Zabotin, the Russian military attaché in Ottawa and a spymaster operating a network of residents and agents widely distributed in the Canadian administration. Ordered to return to Russia, Gouzenko and his wife Anna decided they would prefer to remain in Canada, and as proof of his wish to become a useful Canadian citizen Gouzenko took from the embassy safe all the most secret and damaging documents he could find and handed them over to the Canadian authorities, thus lifting the lid from the hitherto well-sealed box containing the 'atom spies'.

The commotion caused by Gouzenko's defection was profound, mainly because it happened in September 1945, only a few days after the formal Japanese surrender, and at a time when Russia was still regarded by most people in the West as an ally in the war against

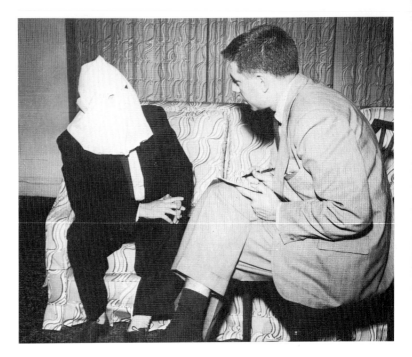

Under the hood is Igor Gouzenko who, shortly after the Japanese capitulation in 1945, revealed the nature and extent of Communist infiltration in the West.

Germany, Italy and Japan. He brought the real Russian threat out into the open, and revealed the nature and extent of Communist infiltration.

A great deal has been written about the best known of the atom spies: the British Alan Nunn May, the German Klaus Fuchs, the Italian Jew Bruno Pontecorvo and, in America, Ethel and Julius Rosenberg. Nunn May was sentenced to ten years' imprisonment, Fuchs to fourteen. Pontecorvo escaped to Russia. The Rosenbergs went to the electric chair.

Nunn May said he had willingly handed over nuclear secrets to Russia because Winston Churchill had been in breach of an agreement to give the Soviet Union all possible technical assistance in fighting the war. Both he and Fuchs tried to make out that physicists, like doctors and surgeons, have a duty to share their knowledge and discoveries for the benefit of all mankind. This, in the context of the two trials, is nonsense – as the learned judges pointed out. Both men had signed the Official Secrets Act and owed allegiance to the British sovereign. Both were ardent Communists, determined that Russia should not be excluded from the 'nuclear powers'. It would be naïve to suppose that, if the situation had been reversed, they would have shared their secrets with Western scientists.

The Fuchs case illustrates one solution to the problem of establishing identity. To wear a red carnation or wait in a certain place may be simple enough, but at the critical moment quite a number of people may be doing the same thing. The Russians allow for coincidence. When Fuchs was instructed to make contact with a man named Raymond, at a street corner on the Lower East Side in New York, he was told to carry a tennis ball. Raymond would be wearing one pair of gloves, carrying another pair, and holding a green book under his arm.

The tracking down of Raymond by the FBI was an extraordinary achievement. Fuchs, in his cell in Wormwood Scrubs in February 1950, told all he knew of the Soviet spy ring working on atomic secrets in the United States, but of Raymond he knew only that this was not his real name, that he was about five feet eight inches tall, weighing around thirteen stone, thick-set and round-faced, with a tendency to shuffle when he walked, and might live somewhere on the East Coast – one man to be found in a population of 170 million.

Initially, the search was concentrated in areas where Raymond and Fuchs had met, for example Santa Fé, where FBI agents called on all hotels, motels, boarding houses and railway, bus and airline offices, checking up on everyone who might fit the description. The most productive leads came from Fuchs's sister and her husband, living in Boston. Fuchs's sister dimly remembered meeting Raymond once – a shortish, stocky man, who talked about chemistry. This started a check of 75,000 firms handling chemical work. Some time later, her husband recalled that Raymond had mentioned Philadelphia, and had spoken about vitamins with apparent knowledge of the subject. Eventually, as the FBI men searched, questioned, checked and cross-checked, a name began to come up with increasing regularity. It was that of a man who fitted the description, a chemist employed in the Philadelphia General Hospital who had been absent from his job on the dates when Fuchs and Raymond had met. Furthermore, he had been the subject of a security check at the time when the FBI was working on another case.

In the end, the nation-wide hunt yielded six possibilities. Photographs were sent to Fuchs, but he failed to recognize any of them. Undeterred, the agents in Philadelphia decided to interview their local suspect and, three months after the search had begun, two agents called on a man named Harry Gold, originally Heinrich Golodnitsky, a Russian immigrant. He claimed he had never been west of the Mississippi, but

Instructions from a Russian spy-handler to one of his operatives, Douglas Ronald Britten, sentenced to 21 years in 1968. Such instructions usually come direct from Moscow – hence the curious English.

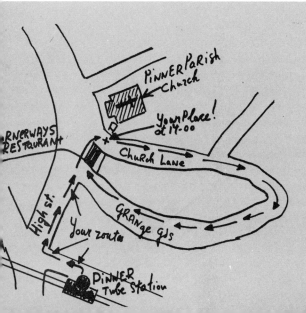

CONSTANT TERMS OF MEETINGS

In case anybody of us fail to come as agreed at previous meeting the following comes into force;

> EVery first saturday beginning from *april of* 1968 you are to come to :

PLACE: „Pinner Parish Church",Church Lane,

> not ar rom"Pinner"underground station, just opposite to the churchs notes-board in the Church Lane

TIME: 14-00hrs and 15-00 hrs,After waiting for 5 minutes you are to go along Church Lane and Grange gdns leading back to the Church.

SIGNS: YOU are to have a book and spectacles in your hands.

PAROLE: „ Could you tell me the way to the local library ? "

YOUR ANSWER:„Unfortunately not. I don't live here."

was trapped by his own lie when a town plan of Santa Fé was found in his bookcase. He then broke down and told them everything.

For obvious reasons security services tend to be reticent about spy-catching. A spy is arrested and a story released to the press, but it seldom contains details of methods or means. Some agents, like Harry Houghton, the clerk employed at the Admiralty Underwater Detection Establishment at Portland, attract suspicion – for a man supposed to be living on a beer income he drank a great deal too much whisky – but the experienced professionals like Colonel Rudolf Abel (whose real name is not known), or an ideologist like Nunn May, an unpaid traitor with unquestioned access to secrets, seldom give themselves away. They are given away. The defector is not a recent acquisition – Rahab defected to the Israelites because she was sure they were going to win – but in the cold war of the twentieth century the defector seems to have a more devastating influence than his predecessors.

Rudolf Abel, who used other names as well, was a colonel in the KGB, and with nearly thirty years of service in Russian espionage behind him he was sent to New York in 1948 to rebuild the structure destroyed by Gouzenko. As Emil R. Goldfus he lived quietly in Brooklyn, and was known as an artist who added photography to his talents as a painter, which were genuine. He played the guitar well, had an insatiable appetite for women, like Sorge, and experimented with radio. Under this cover he built up an organization dealing with nuclear weapons and rocketry, sending his information direct to Moscow by short-wave radio. In 1954 the KGB in Moscow sent him a communications officer named Reino Hayhanen, a member of the Russian Security Police who was also an alcoholic with a grievance. He did not want to be a spy, an illegal 'rezident', but had hoped for a posting to the quiet, safe job of a chauffeur in a foreign embassy. Abel did not trust him, and after some difficulty arranged for him to be recalled. Frightened of what might happen to him when he returned to Moscow, Hayhanen defected.

Abel was arrested. He refused to provide any information and, in October 1957, was sentenced to die in the electric chair – subsequently commuted to thirty years in a penitentiary. In February 1962, however, he was exchanged for Francis Gary Powers, the CIA pilot of the U-2 aircraft shot down into a field near Sverdlovsk on 1 May 1960.

The security services of Russia, America and Britain must by now be accustomed to unpleasant surprises, if only because it is so difficult to expose the intelligent traitor who is not particularly motivated by money and is careful with his contacts, correspondence and communications. It often takes a long time for even the colleagues of a spy to become suspicious, till suddenly the whole case blows wide open and the air is full of recriminations.

Gordon Lonsdale, alias Konon Trofimovich Molody, who ran the Portland spy ring – Harry Houghton and his intimate friend Ethel (Bunty) Gee, and Peter and Helen Kroger alias Cohen – lasted longer than perhaps he should have done. He seems to have been very careless

Rudolf Abel, the highly trained and experienced Russian spy who sent his information on American nuclear weaponry direct to Moscow by short-wave radio.

ЛЕТЧИК СБИТОГО САМОЛЕТА США
ФРЕНСИС ГАРРИ ПАУЭРС

POWERS FRANCIS GARY. THE PILOT OF THE SHOT AMERICAN PLANE

A Soviet exhibition devoted to Gary Powers and the U-2 spy plane, shot down in 1960. Abel was exchanged for Powers in 1962.

in the way he contacted Houghton and Miss Gee, as well as in his visits to the Krogers, who did all the microdot photography and maintained radio communication with Moscow from their bungalow in Ruislip. Yet one can never be sure how much an apparent immunity of this sort is due to the patience of those who know what is going on but, like Walsingham, Thurloe and Vernon Kell, watch and wait until the net is full.

In the case of that strange couple, Sub-Lieutenant Bingham, RN, and Mrs Bingham, it may seem surprising that their hunger for money, their extravagance, and their complete financial irresponsibility did not attract attention. Bingham, driven to the point of collapse by the demands of his Russian handler (Loriy Kuzmin, an assistant naval attaché in the Russian embassy), by his debts, by his duodenal ulcer, and by his hectoring wife, had the choice – as he said himself – of confession, suicide or deeper treachery without being noticed. But this is one of the weaknesses, and, paradoxically, one of the strengths of democracy as opposed to a police state; there is not, as there had been in the time of Thomas Cromwell, a 'scorpion under every stone'.

Though it is doubtful whether accurate figures will ever be obtained, the list of prominent spies, agents and defectors in this cold war is a long one, and the mysteries surrounding some of the names will probably never be solved except within the circle of those who have a 'need to know'. George Blake, for example – a name so English, yet his father's was Behar and he was of Turkish-Spanish-Jewish origin, while his mother was a Dutch girl named Catherine Beijdervellen, of Rotterdam.

Sentenced to forty-two years' imprisonment in 1961, Blake escaped from Brixton prison on 22 October 1966. Was he 'sprung' by the KGB, who try to look after their agents, or was he a double–or perhaps a triple–agent whose trial, sentence and disappearance were all part of the gamesmanship and deception of the secret war?

All the names have a story attached to them: the British Foreign Office employees Guy Burgess and Donald Maclean, for instance, who fled to Russia, warned in time by a mysterious 'third man'. This turned out to be Harold 'Kim' Philby, whose climb up the intelligence ladder had been so swift and successful that at one time it was predicted that he would eventually be the head of MI6. Philby also defected, but he had been under suspicion for some time, and when he disappeared it was from an unimportant assignment in the Middle East. It is imposs-ible for those not in the know to assess the damage done within MI6 by traitors like Blake, Burgess, Maclean and Philby, but the effect of their detection and defection on relationships with organizations such as the CIA can be serious. The discovery in the higher ranks of an intelli-gence organization of so-called ideological spies, who had hitherto appeared to be reasonably intelligent and responsible, is bound to de-stroy confidence and trust.

The list includes the Russian Colonel Oleg Penkovsky, whose infor-mation gave President Kennedy the confidence to call Kruschev's bluff over Cuba and Berlin; William John Christopher Vassall, another Admiralty clerk, who claimed to have been blackmailed by the Rus-sians because of his homosexuality, much as Alfred Redl had been years before; Greville Wynne, who was exchanged for Lonsdale-Molody in 1964; Douglas Britten, Ernst Wollweber, Walter Gramash, Stig Wen-nerström, and Hans and Maria Bammler of the East German intelli-gence service. However, in recalling the cases of those who have gone to Moscow, usually in a great hurry, it must not be forgotten that they are vastly outnumbered by defectors from countries in the Soviet bloc.

When Colonel Pawel Monat, a Polish military attaché, defected to the West, he told America that 'as a country it is rather ingenuous about keeping its secrets'. This is true enough, and applies to most Western democracies. Electronic, aviation and marine publications, trade journals, house magazines of industrial concerns, regimental and corps journals, ordnance maps, tide tables, published data dealing with pho-tography, defence studies and a hundred and one technical subjects provide hostile intelligence services with something in the region of 75 per cent of the information they want–often for an outlay of nothing except time spent in a public library.

The snag is that a democratic society takes pride in having little to conceal from a world it presumes to be reasonably civilized and friendly, whereas the police state, designed to maintain the will of a minority holding the majority in subjection, can exercise far greater control in the name not of freedom but of security.

For thousands of years espionage has been accepted as an unavoid-able element of international relationships. There have always been spies, but whereas in the past the emphasis lay on the man or the woman

as the principal information collection agency, modern technology seems to be making it possible to rely more upon the machine. Much inventive effort is now channelled into the fields of acquisition and dissemination or, in other words, of getting hold of other people's secrets and passing them to those who want them.

We read in our newspapers of 'spy in the sky' satellites with such names as Cosmos, Samos, Midas, Tiros and Nimbus, orbiting the earth with cameras and equipment for monitoring, recording and transmitting, which provide a continuous flow of information. We learn from American sources that the satellite Samos carries cameras which, from heights of 100 miles or more, can focus upon objects only two feet long. At prearranged times cassettes of film and monitoring tape – which record all sorts of things including, sometimes, long-distance telephone calls – are ejected, and collected by Fairchild C-119 Flying Boxcars, helicopters and, if necessary, frogmen. We read, too, of anti-satellite satellites, capable of carrying the secret war to unprecedented heights. We know from incidents like the capture of the spy-ship *Pueblo* by the North Koreans, and from the existence of Russian 'trawlers' with elaborate superstructures, that radio 'ears' are for ever listening. There are cameras which can operate in unlighted rooms, and 'night-viewing' devices which enable people to see long distances in the dark. There is apparatus which records emanations of heat with such definition that an aircraft, flying over the canopy of the jungle, can pinpoint the dying embers of a camp fire or locate a vehicle long after its engine has been switched off.

Kim Philby, defector from the West and former member of MI6, saunters along a Moscow street.

Like the visual microdot for the printed page, radio messages can be condensed into a fraction of a second – known as 'burst transmission'. Microphones can be 'aimed' to pick up the conversation of two people walking together across an open field more than a hundred yards away.

These mechanical gadgets are certainly a great advance on, for instance, the 'sympathetic stain' or the heliograph, but in intelligence there is still very little that is fundamentally new in principle. The satellite is a development of the hot air balloons of the eighteenth century, which added height and range to surveillance, and the function of the balloon was only to take one stage further the instruction Moses gave to his spies: 'Go *up* into the mountain, and see the land.' Radio monitoring is a modern adaptation of young Kerbey's telegraph-tapping in the American Civil War, and this was only the evolution of an ancient practice – waylaying an enemy courier to seize the message he carried. Cryptography had fascinated many minds even before Alexander the Great. The camera is no more than a mechanical means of recording features, buildings or landscapes previously delineated by hand. 'Night-viewing' and other surveillance devices simply extend the functions of the human eye and ear.

It is not easy to foretell what further developments will be made, particularly in acquisition and dissemination, but doubtless they will only be modifications, refinements or improvements on what already exists – intruding even further into the privacy of mankind. They may reduce the risks of espionage by making collection easier and communications more secure, yet, no matter how swiftly, accurately or safely a machine may record information, when applied to espionage it cannot decide what information is to be collected, or how. Nor can it determine the significance of what it records. It cannot be selective; for example, the complex long-range bugging device based on a laser beam is, like most eavesdropping apparatus (including the ear), rendered ineffective by extraneous noise such as radio music in the room where the conversation is being held.

Equipment may become more and more sophisticated, but it can never take the place of the spy, the spymaster or the intelligence officer. 'Glory to Man in the highest,' wrote Swinburne, 'for Man is the master of things.'

No machine can be a substitute for the intellect and ingenuity, courage and resourcefulness the spy must have if he is to penetrate the security defences of the enemy and bring back his secrets; for, as George Washington wrote in a letter to Colonel Elias Dayton on 26 July 1777:

The necessity of procuring good Intelligence is apparent and need not be further urged. All that remains for me to add is that you keep the whole matter as secret as possible. For upon Secrecy, Success depends in most Enterprises of the kind, and for want of it, they are generally defeated, however well planned and promising a favourable issue.

Bibliography

This bibliography is really only a narrow path in the forest of literature on espionage and intelligence. It is arranged alphabetically in eleven sections.

AMERICAN INTELLIGENCE

Bryan, George S., *The Spy in America (1775–1782 & 1861–1865)*, Philadelphia, 1943.

Dulles, Allen, *The Craft of Intelligence*, London, 1963.

Hilsman, Roger, *Strategic Intelligence and National Decision*, Glencoe, Illinois, 1956.

Kane, Harnett T., *Spies for the Blue and the Gray*, New York, 1954.

Kirkpatrick, Lyman B., *The Real CIA*, London, 1968.

Marchetti, Victor L., and Marks, John D., *CIA and the Cult of Intelligence*, London, 1974.

Pennypacker, M., *General Washington's Spies on Long Island and in New York*, L.I. Hist. Soc., 1939.

Powe, Marc B., and Wilson, Edward E., *The Evolution of American Military Intelligence*, US Army Intelligence Center and School, 1973.

Ranson, Harry Howe, *Central Intelligence and National Security*, Cambridge, Massachusetts, 1958.

Smith, R. Harris, *OSS, The History of America's First Central Intelligence Agency*, Berkeley, California, 1972.

Stern, P., *Secret Missions of the Civil War*, Chicago, 1959.

Stewart, Alsop, and Braden, Thomas, *Sub Rosa: The OSS and American Espionage*, New York, 1946.

Yardley, Herbert O., *The American Black Chamber*, London, 1931.

AUTOBIOGRAPHY

Amherst, Jeffrey, Lord, *The Journals*, Canadian Historical Studies, 1931.

Boyd, Belle, *Belle Boyd in Camp and Prison, written by Herself*, New York, 1865.

Brabazon of Tara, Lord, *The Brabazon Story*, London, 1956.

Gleichen, Edward, Lord, *A Guardsman's Memories*, London, 1932.

Leith Hay, Andrew, *A Narrative of the Peninsular War*, London, 1832.

Meinertzhagen, Richard, *Army Diary*, London, 1960.

Moravec, F., *Master of Spies*, London, 1975.

Penkovsky, Oleg, *The Penkovsky Papers*, London, 1965.

Popov, Dusko, *Spy/Counterspy*, London, 1975.

Powers, F. G., *Operation Overflight*, New York, 1970.

Schellenberg, Walter, *Memoirs*, London, 1956.

Vacha, Robert, *A Spy for Churchill*, London, 1975.

Van Deman, Ralph, *Memoirs*, unpublished MS in Library of US Army Intelligence Center and School, Fort Huachuca, Arizona.

BIOGRAPHY

Bernikov, Louise, *Abel*, London, 1970.

Cookridge, J. H., *Gehlen, Spy of the Century*, London, 1971.

Deaken, F. W., and Storry, G. R., *The Case of Richard Sorge*, London, 1966.

Ford, Corey, *Donovan of OSS*, Boston, 1970.

Frazer, Antonia, *Mary Queen of Scots*, London, 1969.

Haswell, Jock (Colquhoun Grant), *The First Respectable Spy*, London, 1969.

Haswell, Jock, *James II, Soldier & Sailor*, London, 1972.

Hohne, Heinz, and Zolting, Hermann, *Network, The Truth about General Gehlen*, London, 1972.

James, Admiral Sir William (Blinker Hall), *The Codebreakers of Room 40*, London, 1952.

Jedlicka, Amorta, *The Canaris File*, London, 1966.

Seth, R., *The Spy Who Wasn't Caught*, London, 1966.

Whiteside, Thomas, *An Agent in Place; The Wennerström Affair*, London, 1967.

BRITISH INTELLIGENCE

Bulloch, John, *MI5*, London, 1963.

Deacon, Richard, *A History of the British Secret Service*, London, 1969.

Haswell, Jock, *British Military Intelligence*, London, 1973.

Henderson, David, Lt.-Col., *Field Intelligence, Its Principles and Practice*, London, 1904.

James, Admiral Sir William, *The Code Breakers of Room 40*, London, 1952.

McLachlan, Donald, *Room 39*, London, 1968.

Masterman, J. C., *The Double Cross System in the War of 1939–45*, London, 1972.

Parritt, Col. B. A. H., *The Intelligencers*, privately printed, Ashford, Kent, 1971.

Winterbotham, F. W., *Secret and Personal*, London, 1974.

Winterbotham, F. W., *Ultra Secret*, London, 1974.

CODES AND CIPHERS

Bond, Raymond T., *Famous Stories of Code and Cipher*, New York, 1947.

Kahn, David, *The Codebreakers*, London, 1966.

Moore, Dan Tyler, and Waller, Martha, *Cloak and Cipher*, London, 1965.

Smith, Lawrence D., *Cryptography – The Science of Secret Writing*, New York, 1955.

THE GREAT WAR (1914–18)

Charteris, Brig-Gen. J., *At GHQ*, London, 1931.

Crutwell, C. R. M. F., *A History of the Great War*, London, 1936.

Falls, Cyril, *The Great War*, London, 1959.

Liddell Hart, B. H., *The Real War*, London, 1930.

HISTORY OF ESPIONAGE

Gramont, Sanche de, *The Secret War; The Story of International Espionage*, London, 1962.

Ind, Col. Allinson, *A Short History of Espionage*, New York, 1963.

Murphy, Brian, *The Business of Spying*, London, 1974.

Rowan, Richard W., and Deindorfer, Robert G., *Secret Service; 33 Centuries of Espionage*, London, 1969.

Seth, Ronald, *Secret Servants; A History of Japanese Espionage*, London, 1957.

Wise, D., and Ross, T., *The Espionage Establishment; Secret Services of the World Powers*, London, 1965.

INDIVIDUAL ESPIONAGE STUDIES

Accoce, Pierre, and Quet, Pierre, *The Lucy Ring*, London, 1967.

Foote, Alexander, *Handbook for Spies*, London, 1964.

Klass, Philip J., *Secret Sentries in Space*, New York, 1971.

Perrault, Giles, *The Red Orchestra*, London, 1967.

Scovell Papers, The, Public Record Office, Reference Number WO 37.

Taylor, J. W. R., and Mondey, David, *Spies in the Sky*, London, 1972.

MISCELLANEOUS SUBJECTS

Delarue, Jacques, *History of the Gestapo*, London, 1964.

Foot, M. R. D., *SOE in France*, London, 1966.

Hamilton, Peter, *Espionage and Subversion in an Industrial Society*, London, 1967.

Heymont, Irving, *Combat Intelligence in Modern Warfare*, Harrisburg, Pa., 1960.

Hinchley, Col. Vernon, *The Defectors*, London, 1954.

Irving, David, *The Mare's Nest*, London, 1964.

Montagu, Ewen, *The Man Who Never Was*, London, 1954.

Roetter, Charles, *Psychological Warfare*, London, 1974.

Sun Tzu, *The Art of War*, ed. Samuel B. Griffith, Oxford, 1963.

Tuchman, Barbara, *The Zimmermann Telegram*, New York, 1958.

Vagts, A., *The Military Attaché*, Princeton, N.J., 1967.

Wohlstetter, Roberta, *Pearl Harbor, Warning and Decision*, Stanford, California, 1962.

RUSSIAN INTELLIGENCE

Barron, John, *KGB*, London, 1974.

Heilbrunn, O., *The Soviet Secret Services*, London, 1956.

Hirsch, Richard, *The Soviet Spies; Russian Espionage in North America*, London, 1948.

SPY STORIES AND CASE HISTORIES

Boveri, Margaret, *Treason in the Twentieth Century*, London, 1961.

Bulloch, J., and Miller, H., *Spy Ring*, London, 1961.

Copeland, Miles, *The Real Spy World*, London, 1974.

Foley, Rae, *Famous American Spies*, New York, 1968.

Franklin, Charles, *Spies of the Twentieth Century*, London, 1967.

Hutton, J. Bernard, *Women Spies*, London, 1971.

Moorehead, Alan, *The Traitors*, London, 1952.

Newman, Bernard, *Spies in Britain*, London, 1964.

Pilat, Oliver, *The Atom Spies*, London, 1954.

Seth, Ronald, *Anatomy of Spying*, London, 1961.

List of Illustrations

Credit line in italics indicates that the photograph was provided by the named museum or other institution.

Index

Page numbers in italics refer to illustrations